THERE IS NOTHING
WRONG WITH YOU

REVISED EDITION

CHERI HUBER

13th printing 2024

Published by Keep It Simple Books
Printed in the United States of America

ISBN 9780971030909

Cover design by Mary Denkinger

Books by Cheri Huber and Ashwini Narayanan
Published by Keep It Simple Books
Making a Change for Good: A Guide to Compassionate Self-Discipline
Don't Suffer, Communicate! A Zen Guide to Compassionate Communication
The Big Bamboozle: How You Get Conned Out of the Life You Want and What to Do about It
What Universe Are You Creating? Zen and the Art of Recording and Listening
I Don't Want To, I Don't Feel Like It: How Resistance Controls Your Life and What to Do about It

Books by Cheri Huber
There Is Nothing Wrong with You: Going Beyond Self-Hate
What You Practice Is What You Have: A Guide to Having the Life You Want
The Fear Book: Facing Fear Once and for All, Rev. Ed.
The Depression Book: Depression as an Opportunity for Spiritual Growth, Expanded and Revised
Transform Your Life: A Year of Awareness Practice
The Key and the Name of the Key Is Willingness
Be the Person You Want to Find: Relationship and Self-Discovery
How You Do Anything Is How You Do Everything, Rev. Ed.
Suffering Is Optional: Three Keys to Freedom and Joy
When You're Falling, Dive: Acceptance, Possibility and Freedom
Nothing Happens Next: Responses to Questions about Meditation
Trying to Be Human: Zen Talks
Sweet Zen: Dharma Talks with Cheri Huber
There Are No Secrets: Zen Meditation with Cheri Huber (DVD)

Unconditional Self-Acceptance: A Do-It-Yourself 6 CD set
Published by Sounds True
How to Get from Where You Are to Where You Want to Be Published by Hay House

Dedication

For Walter,
and for Ramada,
in gratitude

Acknowledgment

My deepest appreciation to everyone who has contributed to this work throughout the years.

Special acknowledgment to all who have participated in our retreats.

Foreword

When I began guiding people along a path of spiritual growth, I realized that much of my role was to be an external representative of the unconditional love and acceptance they were seeking to find in themselves. I also realized early on that they didn't know what they were seeking or that I was playing that role. So we proceeded with the teacher representing the loving, structure-providing mother/father, as well as the wise, compassionate savior who would give them peace, clarity and freedom.

Some quickly concluded that I could not give them what they were looking for and moved on to find someone who could. Others stuck it out, and slowly, step by courageous step, grew to see that no one could give them what they were seeking because it was already theirs, already within them. They found that the work was to realize it for themselves. A teacher could only point the way.

Over the years I've come to see that what I'm doing as a guide is trying to get folks to turn loose the conditioning that says they are bad, wrong and inadequate long enough to catch a glimpse of who they really are. It is only after years of learning to trust my perceptions that they begin to accept the possibility that their beliefs about themselves and their world might be less than completely accurate.

Every spiritual path tells us that what we are seeking is inside us. When we are children we learn to stop looking to ourselves to know what is so for us and to begin turning to others to know what is right. We learn to look first to parents, then to teachers, friends, lovers, husband or wife, children, Jesus or the Buddha or God—all "out there." The love, the acceptance, the approval is out there and must be earned somehow.

Once we have completed the turn away from ourselves, away from our heart, we experience ourselves as separate and find ourselves in a fight for survival. I am now a small self, adrift in a threatening world. My focus must be on surviving.

Society offers us help in the form of various techniques and processes designed to enable us to cope better. But some of us, I would say the lucky ones, can't learn to cope. We keep having a nagging, unsettling sense that there is something fundamentally wrong with the whole structure. "It's not just that I'm wrong. It feels bigger than that."

This deep down dissatisfaction will sometimes lead a person to consider the realm of the spirit. "Maybe it's even bigger than I thought."

The reason spiritual practice is essential in doing the work of going beyond self-hate is that to be free of self-hate we must find the Unconditional. We might not have the words or concepts, but what we are longing for is something greater than this world, something lasting and secure. Of course, egocentricity (the illusion that you are separate from everything else) begins by thinking it can find this for itself. But, initially, that doesn't matter. It's the looking that matters, not who is looking or what is being looked for.

Egocentricity is conditional. It is dualistic. It is the process of believing oneself to be separate. The illusion of separateness is not capable of experiencing wholeness.

A spiritual practice, if we are willing and patient and sincere, will eventually lead us to that which can embrace the egocentric, conditioned belief in separateness.

As you learn to sit down, sit still and pay attention, you begin to glimpse that which sees through the illusion, beyond the voices of society's conditioning, back to the original being. And slowly that perceiving becomes more real than all you've been taught to believe. You begin to cease identifying with the small, frightened, socialized, conditioned person you always thought was the real you and you gain a much broader view.

With practice, you will move from being one who is hoping and looking to be saved to that which can save. You will begin to be the love, acceptance and compassion you have always sought.

In lovingkindness,
Cheri

Table of Contents

You have been taught
that there is something wrong with you
and that you are imperfect,
but there isn't
and you're not.

Surviving Childhood: Establishing a Strong, Early Foundation for Self-Hate

Unless you were raised by wolves, the chances are extremely good that as you were growing up, you heard at least a few of the following:

Don't do that...Stop that...Put that down... I told you not to do that...Why don't you ever listen...Wipe that look off your face...I'll give you something to cry about...Don't touch that...You shouldn't feel that way...You should have known better...Will you ever learn...You should be ashamed of yourself...Shame on you...I can't believe you did that...Don't ever let me see you do that again...See, that serves you right...I told you so...Are you ever going to get it...What were the last words out of my mouth...What were you thinking of...You ruin everything...You have no sense...You're nuts...The nurses must have dropped you on your head...Just once, do something right...I've sacrificed everything for you and what thanks do I get...I had great hopes for you...If I've told you once, I've told you a thousand times...Give you an inch, you take a mile...Anybody would know that...Don't talk back to me...You'll do as you are told...You're not funny...Who do you think you are...Why did you do it that way...You were born bad...You drive me crazy...You do that just to hurt me...I could skin you alive...What will the neighbors say...You do that to torture me...You're so mean...I could beat the daylights out of you...It's all your fault...You make me sick...You're trying to kill me...Now what's the matter with you, cry baby...Go to your room...You deserve it...Eat it because children are starving...Don't stick your lip out...If you cry, I'll slap you...Don't you ever think about anyone else...Get out of my sight...

and on and on
          and on and on.

Somewhere along the line, you concluded that there was something wrong with you.

OF COURSE YOU DID!
WHAT ELSE COULD YOU CONCLUDE?

IF THERE WERE NOTHING
WRONG WITH YOU,
PEOPLE WOULDN'T
TREAT YOU THAT WAY!

THEY WOULDN'T SAY
THOSE THINGS TO YOU!

"Then why did they do that to me?"

Because it was done to them.
Because we do
what we've been taught.

Society calls this
"child rearing"
or
"socialization."

We call it
"sad."

The process of socialization teaches us:

- to assume there is something wrong with us
- to look for the flaws in ourselves
- to judge the "flaws" when we find them
- to hate ourselves for being the way we are
- to punish ourselves until we change

We've been taught that this is what good people do.

Socialization does not teach us:

- to love ourselves for our goodness
- to appreciate ourselves for who we are
- to trust ourselves
- to have confidence in our abilities
- to look to our heart for guidance

We've been taught that this is "self-centered."

By the time "socialization" is complete,
most of us hold an

that our only hope of being good is to
punish ourselves when we are bad.

We believe beyond doubt that without

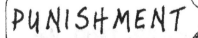

bad would win out over good.

This entire book
is based on the premise
that that is not true!

Here's what's possible:

Child
is
born.

Child learns to
turn away from
self toward other
to get needs met
(stops trusting
intuitive knowing).

Child
is
reborn.

Need is not met;
child believes it is
because s/he is bad.
Child abandons self and
decides to be perfect
(be who others want).
"I won't need anything."
"I shouldn't be afraid."
"I'll do everything right."

Person finds
compassion and
self-acceptance.

Awareness
Practice

Person tries
everything to
make conditioning
work.

Child begins to develop
survival behaviors that are
self-denying, self-preserving,
self-destructive (ex: shuts
down emotionally, eats to
stuff feelings, etc.).

Suffering

Older, person uses self-hating
behaviors to try to be a good
person (values others over
self, denies self, uses ideals
against self).

My Survival System Is Killing Me!

What *happened* to you, not who you are,
makes you angry, fearful, greedy, mean,
anxious, etc.

We learned behaviors when we were very
young in order to survive. We were taught
to hate those behaviors and to see them as
signs of our badness. Yet we must keep
doing them because they still mean survival
to us.

And we hate ourselves for doing them.

THE TRAP:
 I believe I must be this way to survive.
 I hate myself for being this way.

RESULT:
 self-hate = survival
 survival = self-hate

Suffering provides our identity.

Identity is maintained in struggle and dissatisfaction, in trying to fix what's wrong.

So we are constantly looking for what is wrong, constantly creating new crises so we can rise to the occasion. To ego, that's survival.

It is very important
that something be wrong
so we can continue to survive it.

Self-Hate Is a Process.

Self-hate is a "how" not a "what." Examples:

If I'm a worrier, worrying is the "how," the process. The things I worry about are the "whats," the content.

If I am judgmental, judging is the "how," the process. The things I judge are the "whats," the content.

If I am caught in self-hate, self-hating is the "how," the process. The aspects of "me" that are being hated—body, personality, looks (the list is endless)—are the "whats," the content.

In other words, I am not hating myself, self-hate is hating me. Self-hate is an autonomous process with a life of its own, an endless recorded loop of conditioning, creating and shaping the world in which we live.

The simplest example is that if self-hate is hating my body,

it doesn't matter what I do or what I look like, I will never meet self-hate's standard,

which is the point.

Self-hate is not hating me
to help me.

No. It is a process of hating,
and hating is just
what it does.

As long as it exists,
it will find something to hate!

That's how it maintains itself.

The process of self-hate
is so much a part
of the average person
that we don't even recognize it.

We think we're just
doing the things that
will ensure we'll be good.

It's normal, we say.
Everybody does it,
or should.

If you want to know what you were conditioned to believe as a child, look at the self-criticism that goes through your head now...*

Does that mean someone consciously, deliberately treated you that way?

Perhaps not.

But you got the message anyway,
                                    didn't you?

*Even if the voice says "I," the implication is "you."

A Scam Self-Hate Loves to Run

It is confusing for someone to conclude that they aren't loved because there is something wrong with them.

"I want to be loved, but there's something wrong with me. I need to fix that even though I'm not really sure I know what it is or how to fix it. But I must keep trying anyway because I really want to be loved."

This person who is trying to become lovable spends much time, attention, and energy trying to be good, earn approval, please others,

BE PERFECT.

And then, when they find that all that trying to be good doesn't work, and doesn't in fact get the love and approval they want, the only thing they know how to do is

TRY HARDER.

It's like being on a journey
and being completely lost,

going in the wrong direction
but making really good time.

And what we are left with is confusion. "I'm trapped and confused. What I'm doing isn't working, but I don't know what to do instead." Confusion is the result of attempting to cling to a conditioned belief (if I try harder I can make it work) in the face of what you are seeing to be true for you (this isn't working, I feel powerless, there must be another way).*

If you will continue to pay attention, the confusion will give way to clarity. If you can find the willingness to LOOK, AND TAKE A STAND AGAINST THE SCAM SELF-HATE HAS YOU CAUGHT IN, the confusion will give way to clarity.

And the clarity is compassion.

---

*It's always a good idea to go back and check out the original premise. The faulty premise in this case is that if you meet the endless, changing, nebulous list of conditioning's standards, you will be who you should be, you will be lovable, and you will be loved.

Some of the Forms Self-Hate Takes

SABOTAGE
You try to do something good for yourself
or for someone else and somehow manage
to turn the whole thing against yourself.
You keep doing the very things you didn't
want to do or don't approve of, and you
can't seem to figure out how you do that.
It's a perfect system for self-hate because:
1. You're operating out of an ideal.
2. You don't live up to the ideal.
3. You can't figure out what you're doing
wrong.

TAKING BLAME BUT NOT CREDIT
If something goes well, it's a gift from God.
If it goes badly, it's all your fault. And even
if you do take a little credit for something,
you can always avoid feeling good about it by
finding what could have been done better.

BLAMING OTHERS
Self-hating and "other"-hating are the same thing. Whether you are hateful toward others or hating yourself directly, it's self-hate. You are always the recipient.

BEING SECRETIVE
You don't let people know what's going on inside you so that you can be in there being beaten.

HOLDING GRUDGES
You review old hurts and injustices rather than being present to yourself now.

NOT BEING ABLE TO RECEIVE
Gifts, favors, help, praise, etc., are things you have difficulty allowing yourself to have.

SEEING WHAT IS WRONG
Your habit is to find fault, criticize, judge and compare. Remember, what is is all that is. The alternate reality in which everything is as you think it should be exists only in your mind, and it exists primarily to torture you.

TRYING TO BE DIFFERENT
Being who you are, your "plain old self," isn't enough. You feel you have to maintain an image.

BEING ACCIDENT PRONE
Your attention is so often focused on some other time, person or thing that you injure yourself in the present. You don't feel you deserve your attention. Others are more important.

PUTTING YOURSELF IN ABUSIVE SITUATIONS
Even if you realize that you have this pattern, your fear and self-hate are too strong to let you break out of it.

MAINTAINING AN UNCOMFORTABLE PHYSICAL POSITION
You hold your shoulders in a way that creates pain. You clench your teeth. You "sit small" on the bus so as not to intrude into anyone else's space. You continue to

sit in an uncomfortable chair at work
because you don't want to make waves.

MAINTAINING AN UNCOMFORTABLE MENTAL POSITION

Clinging to "shoulds": "It's not right to be
happy when there is so much suffering in
the world." "People should say please and
thank you." "Children deserve to have two
parents."

ATTEMPTING TO BE PERFECT

This one speaks for itself.

Some Voices and Gestures and Actions of Self-Hate

A word or gesture can conjure up a whole lifetime of negativity or defeat or unworthiness. When the memories and emotions tied to that word or gesture arise, it's like having a truckload of self-hate dumped on you.

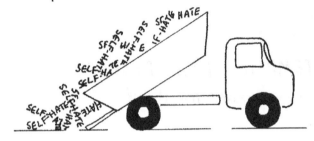

"I can't believe you did that!"

"God, Cheryl!" (tone of disgust)

A shrug of the shoulders and the words "It doesn't matter." (signals total defeat)

A sinking feeling of "I've done something wrong" and a feeling of panic, "What's the right thing to do now to fix it?"

Buying anything for anyone else but never anything for myself.

Wanting to eat something and a voice saying, "Can't you ever say no to yourself?" and realizing that I say no to myself all the time about everything except food.

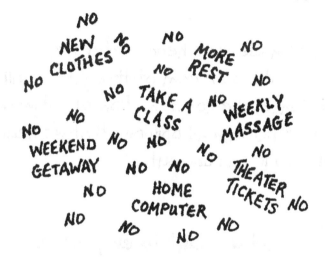

The Voices

By way of explanation...
In this book we refer often to "the voices inside your head" or similar phrases.

We aren't talking about a psychological disorder.

"Voices inside your head" refers to the nearly endless stream of thoughts we all experience, the constant flow of judgments, ideas, criticism, and opinions that we hear inside day in and day out.

**And we want to emphasize
that it is important
not to believe that these "voices"
have helpful information for you
about yourself.**

So far in this book we have been defining self-hate for you.

So, what is egocentricity?

Egocentricity is the illusion of being a separate self, separate from everything— ourselves, each other, life, the universe— that results primarily from the process of social conditioning.

Egocentricity is interested in one thing and one thing only: ITS SURVIVAL AT ANY COST.

IT WILL SAY AND DO ANYTHING
to remain in control of your life.
It will come through any door.
It will stop at nothing.

Self-hate has many voices.
Here are a few.

VOICE: Nothing subtle about it.
"You're disgusting. You make me sick."

VOICE: Sounds like normal, helpful, constructive criticism.
"It was stupid of me to have said that. I must watch what I say." (Children learn early to call themselves and others "stupid.")

VOICE: Sounds like self-discipline; helpful in keeping us on the right track.
"I must finish this now even though I'm exhausted. I must not give in to little self-indulgences. Who knows where it would stop?"

VOICE: Sounds really, really true and helpful; the voice of clarity and wisdom.
You read a book that is meaningful for you, but every sentence is translated into "I should be like that." This voice might start

out sounding sincere but soon slides into accusation. "I've been doing it wrong all this time. What's wrong with me?" Another example: Sitting in meditation you might be quiet and comfortable, just breathing. Then a voice says, "I don't think I'm doing this right. If I were, my attention wouldn't wander."

You can listen to the voices that say
there is something wrong with you.

It's actually very helpful
to be aware of them.

Just don't believe them!

Most of what we have been

TAUGHT TO BELIEVE

we had to be

TAUGHT TO BELIEVE

BECAUSE

IT ISN'T TRUE!

This is why children have to be conditioned so heavily! WE WOULD NEVER HAVE REACHED THESE CONCLUSIONS ON OUR OWN!

If we could for a moment look at what we've been taught to believe with an unconditioned mind, we would see that not only is it not true,

it's absurd.

"Where did all

this self-hate

come from?"

Socialization and Aspects of the Personality

We learn self-hate as children, and we learn it whether we grow up in a loving family or not.
The steps go pretty much like this.

1.

The child has a need.

EXAMPLE:
The child is afraid of the dark and wants to be comforted.

2.

The need is rejected.

Her parents say: "You are a bad girl to be out of bed! Go back to bed this instant!"

3.

The child comes up with a behavior as a means of survival in order to get the need met.

For example, being afraid of the dark, she/he will sneak a flashlight into bed.

4.

The child simultaneously identifies with the authority figure who didn't meet the need ("They're right, I'm bad for being this way."), and identifies with the part who was rejected ("I'm afraid, and they don't love me because I'm afraid.")

The child, completely incapable of grasping any of this consciously, nevertheless learns to believe: "There must be something wrong with me. That's why they are treating me this way. It's my fault. It's not their fault." In the child's mind there can't be anything wrong with the parents because survival depends on them.

THIS IS THE BIRTH OF SELF-HATE.

5.

The child decides to be "perfect," to do everything right, to be really good in order to be loved. There is no choice about this; the child's survival depends on it.

"They don't love me because there is something wrong with me. I have to think of everything. If I just do it right and never let that happen again, then they'll love me."

THIS CONVERSATION MAINTAINS SELF-HATE.

6.

To ensure survival, "The Judge" as an aspect of the personality is born to make sure that the child is perfect and right and good.

The birth of The Judge guarantees the continued existence of self-hate.

This process repeats constantly up through age 7 when, it is said, we are completely socialized. After that, The Judge is tenured and guaranteed a full-time job.

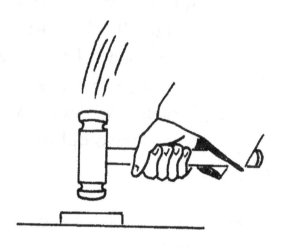

During this process we have concluded that needs are bad and that we are bad for having them.

And, of course, we have them anyway.

Why Am I So Needy?

STUDENT: Recently you used the term "horrible, needy thing," and I realized that's exactly how I think of it: needy is horrible. No wonder I can't let neediness come up in myself. And when I see it in others, I slam them down with the same judgment that it's horrible and unacceptable.

HORRIBLE
NEEDY
THING

GUIDE: That's an example of the conclusion we drew when we first began learning to abandon ourselves. We concluded that the reason we were being rejected was that we had a need, and having a need means you're bad. If you're bad, you're unlovable, and if you're unlovable you won't be able to survive. So from that perspective, the bottom line is

Don't Have Needs.

Once we turn our attention outward, most of us never address the original unmet need we were traumatized into abandoning.

Most of us don't know that it is that original unmet need that has been

controlling our lives.

The need?
To be loved
    and accepted
        exactly as we are.

Eventually it dawns on us that we can't stay in the "I'm wrong" mode forever or we really won't survive. There has to be a duality formed in which "I'm not wrong, they are wrong" operates.

The sadness is that you can live your whole life trying to prove your parents wrong, but nothing will really have changed. All your ideas about being perfect and right and good will just be in reaction to the conditioning you received from your parents. Not only will you pursue those ideas of perfection, but eventually you will have to reject them, and you will have to reject them perfectly, and pretty soon you will have tied yourself up in such a knot that you won't be able to move in any direction, and you will just sit there in self-hate because the bottom line is

you lose.

Self-Hate Accounting:
The "Insufficient Funds" Rule

 STUDENT: Why do I never feel that I have been good enough and generous enough? I try and try but this little nagging guilty feeling is always here.

GUIDE: Good question. I look at this a lot. It's just so pervasive in human experience. I was talking about it earlier and gave this example: You go along in life and you do what you're supposed to do. And every time you do something you're supposed to do, you put a dollar in the bank. Okay. Every time you're kind, patient, or you do the thing you're supposed to do—whatever it is (you know what those things are for you)—every time, you put a dollar in the bank, a dollar in the bank, a dollar in the bank...

DEPOSITS

And you're working at this! You're up early in the morning, doing these things until late at night. Every day.

Finally, you feel like you're just kind of worn out. You feel like you need a little pleasure in your life, a little time on the beach or something. And so you think, "I'm going to go to the bank, and I'm going to take out some money, and I'm going to do something nice for myself."

So you go to the bank and you say, "Here I am. I want to take out some of the money I've saved so that I can do something nice for myself."

And the response is, "Oh no. You haven't earned nearly enough to get anything for yourself. Oh, you have to work much harder. You have to put much, much more money in before you can get anything for yourself."

REQUEST DENIED

REASON: INSUFFICIENT FUNDS

Of course, if this were First National you were dealing with you would say, "No, this is not the way this is going to work. This is my money. You can't tell me when and where and how I can spend it." And yet, at the Bank of Self-Hate, that's exactly the way it works!

With self-hate you get to earn and earn and earn endlessly, and there is never a payback. You think that you're saving up all these points and that someday you'll receive some benefit from them, BUT YOU NEVER WILL.

STUDENT: Yes, that happens a lot.

GUIDE: Let me give you another example. You decide that you're going to take up running. And so this person is going to help you become a runner. You put on your little outfit and the person says,

"Why'd you put that on? You're going to wear that? Boy, do you look stupid!"

Well, you go put on another outfit—you put on several outfits and finally just give up on that discussion.

You're never going to look good enough to run so you just decide you're going to do it anyway.

You go out there and start running, and the person says, "You call that running? Do you really think you can be a runner?"

Now, I just want to give you another possibility, okay? How about if the person who is with you says, "Run in anything, it doesn't matter. You look fine. Just get out there and run. That's great! You're doing good. How long did you run? Ten minutes? That's wonderful!"

Think about it!
Which person wants you to run,
and which person wants you not to run?

THERE'S NO MYSTERY IN THIS, FOLKS!

It's not hard to pick out which characters are in which camp. Internally or externally! In the first example, the person at the Bank of Self-Hate DOES NOT LIKE YOU!

It's important to get that!

It's not like this person is really pulling for you to get enough money in the bank to do something special for yourself.

NO!
This person
        will never
                give you
                        a dime!

You will work yourself to death, and you'll never get a thing for it. It is really important to understand that!

If you had a person
in your life

treating you the way
you treat yourself,

you would have gotten rid of them

a long

time

ago.

STUDENT: You'd think so, wouldn't you?

GUIDE: It seems so clear, but because that voice speaks from inside our own head, we are actually willing to perpetuate the illusion that this person:
-- is on our side
-- likes us
-- has something valuable to say
-- has some sort of merit in life.

But it doesn't!
It is a pathetic thing.

It does not need to be
in charge of anybody's life.

And so you don't let it run your life.
You don't let it sign on your bank account.
You don't let it arrange your calendar.
You don't even let it cook for you.

Are you with me?

STUDENT: I am with you. Sometimes I don't see that separation. Right now, right here in this room, it seems very clear to me.

GUIDE: I can give you the simplest of all possible rules of thumb: Anytime a voice is talking to you that is not talking with love and compassion, don't believe it!

Even if it is talking about someone else, don't believe it. Even if it is directed at someone else, it is the voice of self-hate. It is simply hating you through an external object. It can hate you directly by telling you what a lousy, rotten person you are, and it can hate you indirectly by pointing out what's wrong "out there."

If the voice is not loving,
don't listen to it,
don't follow it,
don't believe it.

No exceptions!

Even if it says it's "for your own good,"
it is not. It's for its good, not yours. This is
the same as when parents talk to you in a
hateful tone of voice "for your own good."
It's for their good. It makes them feel
better. It does not make you better. And
it does not make you behave "better."

Here are some outrageous things I
suggest about this. Anytime you hear the
voice of self-hate, do something for
yourself that will make it crazy.

Buy yourself a present.
Sit down and read for pleasure.
Take a long, hot bath.

STUDENT: Whatever it is that you can't let yourself do.

GUIDE: Yes. Whatever would be lazy and indulgent.

STUDENT: Thoughtless, selfish...

GUIDE: <u>YES!</u> The more, the better. It can be as simple as going for a walk on a nice day. You just keep walking until the voice is still, until it is clear that it's not in control anymore. Then, when you're ready, when you're present, go back to your regular life.

Constructive Criticism: Not Required

Let's say that you sense you have been less than kind toward someone.

The voice of "constructive criticism" says quietly, "That was pretty harsh. You're too sarcastic. You always have been. You better clean up your act before you alienate everyone."

This voice justifies itself by saying things like,

"I'm just trying to point these things out to you so that you'll be a better, kinder, happier person."

"Constructive criticism" is a scam
run by people who want
to beat you up.
And they want you to believe
that they're doing it
for your own good!

BE SUSPICIOUS of any voice, inside or outside, that says there is something wrong with you. This voice does not like you and is not helpful. It is possible that with the awareness that you have been unkind toward someone, you might realize, in a gentle sort of way, "I don't want to do that. It doesn't feel very good." And it's not that you're a bad person, or even that you shouldn't be that way; it's just that you don't want to be unkind because it hurts your heart.

When you are open to that awareness,
you won't need to try to be different,
for in that gentle approach
you will already have changed.

COMMON WISDOM
that supports self-hate

It is more blessed to give than to receive.

You can't teach an old dog new tricks.

The lyrics to "Santa Claus Is Coming to Town"

You get what you deserve.

The harder you try, the better you'll do.

Two heads are better than one.

Some things are just meant to be.

If you are not the lead dog, the view never changes.

Children should be seen and not heard.

Do as I say, not as I do.

ADD YOUR OWN:

CONFLICTING BELIEFS
that maintain self-hate

Patience is a virtue.
Strike while the iron is hot.

I am my brother's keeper.
Look out for Number One.

Neither a borrower nor a lender be.
Generosity is a virtue.

Carpe diem. (Seize the day.)
Save for a rainy day.

Be realistic.
Be imaginative.

Express yourself.
Control yourself.

ADD YOUR OWN:

Self-Evaluation: Another Unhelpful Idea

Self-hate is

LIFE'S LITTLE
REPORT CARD

DOING IT RIGHT	A+
BEING ATTENTIVE	A+
MAKING DECISIONS	A+
HELPING OTHERS	A+
BEING SUCCESSFUL	A+
HANDLING PRESSURE	D-

putting incredible pressure on myself
to be perfect,
which causes me to make mistakes*
because I'm so stressed
and overwhelmed
and miserable.

*It isn't actually possible to make mistakes

Investing in Misery

 STUDENT: I tend to focus on punishment and not notice reward. I seem to believe that punishment works and reward doesn't. I wonder what I get from having this belief.

GUIDE: If you believe that punishment works, then it makes sense to do a bunch of stuff you consider wrong so you can be punished a lot and life will "work" according to your beliefs.

STUDENT: It seems I'm invested in misery.

GUIDE: Keep in mind that egocentricity, self-hate, and misery are synonymous. To be miserable is to be the center of the universe.

Now let's add the ingredient of knowing I've done something wrong, but turning it around so that I am the victim and should be compensated. "Yes I embezzled money from the company, but the owners are filthy rich and I deserve more than I get for working so long and hard for them. They owe me." "I know I didn't get the project done on time, but my life is really hard and they shouldn't have fired me. I think I'll sue them for wrongful termination."

Isn't that perfect? Even our misdeeds are used to ego's advantage.

And then, of course, ego is usually right there with suggestions to make up for injustices—large or small—that we feel we've suffered. Things like:
-- rationalizing dishonesty
-- spurious legal actions
-- not returning a wallet you find
-- having an affair with someone's partner
-- driving discourteously
-- gossiping
-- ice cream
"After all, life owes me something for this injustice."

Self-Hate Accounting System

In the self-hate accounting system:

-- I add up everything I do. I subtract everything everyone else doesn't do.

-- I add up everything everyone else gets. I subtract everything that I don't get.

-- I add up all the luck everybody else has. I subtract all the luck I don't have.

-- I add up all the advantages everybody else had. I subtract all the advantages I didn't have.

You get the picture.

I am so far in the hole because all I do is good things and all I get is bad things.

So, how can I not feel myself to be a victim?
And why should I not try to even the score?

And, of course, we fail to see that almost everyone sees themselves as victims and others as victimizers. And we continue to victimize one another.

Who of us will stop?

Self-Hate and the Battering Cycle

In adult relationships, the stresses of life can lead one partner to become physically or verbally abusive toward the other. This can result in a cyclical pattern of behavior that includes the following elements: increasing stress, abuse, contrition, and a decision to "be perfect."

We often think of the battering cycle happening between a man and a woman, but it can happen with any two or more people. In the form of self-hate, it requires only oneself.

In the classic situation, a man and a woman get together because they want to make their lives better. He will take care of her, and she will be supportive to enable him to take care of her.

After a while, it stops working. The stresses of life push him to a crisis point, and he relieves his frustration by beating her. Then he feels good because his stress is relieved, but he feels bad because he beat his wife.

She feels good because she's been punished for letting him down, but she feels bad because her husband just beat her.

Then they get together and decide that this awful thing must never happen again, and they both feel better.

They have a plan. It's under control. "We won't make that mistake again. We'll do better. We'll be perfect."

And the stress begins to build again...

Addictive behaviors—whether it's food, alcohol, drugs, sex, smoking, work, relationships—follow the same cycle.

FOR EXAMPLE:

The stresses of life begin to build, and I reach for my addiction of choice. If it's food, I head for the kitchen and eat my way from one end to the other.

I feel good because the stress is relieved. I have kind of anesthetized myself, and the craving is calmed. But I feel AWFUL because I have just eaten a ton!

So I submit to self-hate's beatings
until I'm convinced
that I've got a grip on it.

I see what happened.
It will never happen again.
I have a program.
I've got it right this time.
I'm going to do better.
In fact, I'll be perfect.

And the stress

begins to build...

THE BATTERING CYCLE

STRESS

And the
pressure to
be perfect
leads to...

Stress overload
leads to...

DECISION
TO BE
PERFECT
(I will never
beat, abuse,
etc., again!)

COPING
BEHAVIORS
(getting beaten,
eating, abusing
substances,
etc.)

These same
behaviors lead
to feeling worse.
(I did it again!)

These behaviors
lead to feeling
better (reward).

FEEL BETTER
then
FEEL WORSE

This process can happen between two people
or within ourselves, between two aspects of
the personality.

Adopting the belief that you must be
perfect is the perfect set up for self-hate.
You believe that your choices are to be
perfect or to be a failure.
BUT SELF-HATE SETS THE STANDARD
OF PERFECTION
and you can bet you are never
going to meet that standard.

If you did, if you met that standard, what
would self-hate beat you with? What would
it frighten you with? And if you weren't
frightened, how would you be controlled?

Self-hate would have you believe that either
it is in control, making you be who and how
you should be, or not only will you be
imperfect, you will be garbage.

 It has convinced you that if
you were to be just how you
are, you would be awful.

So, the
BIG, UGLY LIE
becomes a
BIG, UGLY BELIEF:

Self-hate,
 judgment,
  blame,
   punishment,
    and rejection

are all for your benefit because they're the only things keeping you from being

A TERRIBLE PERSON.
(Have we made our point?)

Would you please risk it and find out once and for all how you are WITHOUT the beatings and abuse?

Spiritual Practice Doesn't Begin Until the Beatings Stop.

I'm suggesting that you stop the beatings. Many spiritual teachers suggest that hatred is not the answer. They say things about love, forgiveness, generosity and gratitude. They hardly talk about beating people and hating people and this sort of thing. They say, "Now, folks, this is the direction. This is the way to go. If you really want to wake up and end your suffering and find joy and peace and bliss, this is the way to do it." And the response is, "Nah, I don't think so. I'm not going to do that."

So, here's the deal. If you were to, say for instance, find the willingness to stop the beatings for just one day, and if you turned into a more hideous person than you are now, the next day you could submit to twice the beatings and catch up. I'm just suggesting that you might consider taking the risk.

 GUIDE: It takes a tremendous amount of courage to stop the beatings. I suspect it's not because we really think we'll be bad if we do. I suspect it's because we don't want to come up against what conditioning and self-hate are going to try to do to us if we take control of our lives.

If you decide that you are no longer going to be intimidated by the beatings, you will be immediately engaged in a life and death struggle because the moment that "stick" is taken away . . . think about it! If you aren't threatened with punishment, what will drive you to succeed? To make those phone calls? To make that list? To get through that list? And what will happen if you don't do the things you're supposed to do?

VARIOUS STUDENTS: "My life will go down the tubes." "I'll be accused of being irresponsible." "I'll lose that image I have of myself." "People will see through me." "I'll feel guilty."

GUIDE: It'll get so bad that you'll just die.

STUDENT: I think that's what it would eventually come to. If I don't do my work, and don't make money, then I won't be able to pay for my house, and I won't have any food. And if I follow that along far enough, I realize that I believe that all those things on the list are designed to keep me alive. And if I don't do them the ultimate consequence is death.

GUIDE: That's what happens, isn't it? Do this task or die (laughter). Even if it's get a haircut today. What if you found out that voice had no power over you at all? What if you didn't believe that you were going to die if you didn't do what it told you to do?

STUDENT: I think I would just do the next thing on the list. The belief is that I need the beatings. I need the fear of death to do all of these things. I believe it's that drive that keeps me working and doing things.

GUIDE: So, what would happen if you stopped believing the voices of self-hate? What would happen to you if you stopped the beatings?

ANOTHER STUDENT: I find that the worst beatings don't come about my list of things to do. They're about behavior, psychological kinds of things and emotional ways that I have learned I'm supposed to be, as if they are the laws of the universe. I must be polite in these circumstances. I must be nice or clever or whatever it is.

GUIDE: So, you come home after an evening out during which you've said something unfortunate. What would happen if you didn't respond to that with self-hate?

STUDENT: I have tried it. I've had some success, and it does seem to require terrific energetic awareness, every second. It takes a huge amount of being present. And it takes courage because it feels so much like it is the good person thing to do to scold myself for what I've done.

GUIDE: Yet, what you're describing is not scolding.

STUDENT: It's worse than that.

GUIDE: It's abuse. That's what you're really describing. And so, the "good person" thing to do is to submit to the abuse. Pretty weird, huh?

STUDENT: There seems to be an element of not having control and/or giving up control. If I don't get a beating, there's a feeling of spaciousness, and at the same time a terror of that spaciousness. Part of me wants more than anything not to be in control, to just go with the moment, to flow with the process. Another part clings desperately to control, wants to know what's going to happen, wants to like what happens and to influence what happens. But what comes out most for me is this one that's just terrified.

GUIDE: But not terrified of abuse, terrified of the lack of it, of the spaciousness.

STUDENT: No beatings creates an uncomfortable sense of total freedom.

GUIDE: Freedom and spaciousness, that's what's there. It's also a loss of identity because identity is maintained through this insanity we're describing. That's what keeps me at the center of the universe. That's what keeps the whole thing going. If I learn to pay attention, to be present in the moment, I can see all of this happening.

Meditation: Feel the Burn

If I am practicing meditation, I am growing daily, one hopes, accustomed to spaciousness, to a feeling of freedom. I'm practicing coming back to the present, to center. I wander off; I drop it; I come back. Wander off...drop it...come back. Over and over I realize that nothing goes wrong and nothing happens to me. I'm perfectly fine.

If you're ever going to be free, you must be willing to prove to yourself that your inherent nature is goodness, and that when you stop doing everything else, goodness is what's there. You'll never prove that to yourself as long as you're indulging the beatings, as long as you think the only thing making you a good person is the beatings.

At some point, if you're sincerely going to pursue spiritual practice, you must find the courage to stop the beatings for long enough to find out that what you are is goodness.

This is why we have a meditation practice: to learn to sit still with whatever is happening. **There isn't anything in any of it. It's just stuff.** It's just what we're hooked into, what we're identified with, what we're clinging to in order to try to maintain the illusion of ourselves as separate beings; it's all that scrambling that we're conditioned to do. Something goes wrong, someone disapproves of us, or we disapprove of ourselves, and we go into high gear to try to make it right so that we can get everything put back together.

When we sit still in meditation, we don't scratch if we have an itch. Now, this drives people crazy. I've had people say, "This is demented. How could not scratching when you itch have anything to do with spiritual practice?" It has everything to do with spiritual practice because it's that "It itches, I must scratch" reaction that is at the root of most of our suffering.

But you can just notice that it itches (ah, itching) and not have to do anything about it. You can realize that you are having a conditioned reaction to a sensation. You don't have to take it personally. You don't have to react to it.

If you learn once that you don't have to react that way, you're free of it. You prove to yourself that you won't die and you won't go crazy and parts of your body won't fall off. You can just be there and be perfectly fine. Then something hurts and you can sit through that. It just becomes interesting. You're not resisting it any more. It's just kind of fascinating how it hurts there, and pretty soon it hurts here, and then it doesn't hurt at all.

And then you think, "You know, my leg was hurting." You're sitting there quietly, breathing in, breathing out, and this "helpful" little voice says, "Wasn't your leg hurting a little while ago?" Suddenly, you're in pain again. So we learn to sit still with that.

Maybe you're obsessing about something. The voice says, "You know, I can't sit here. I can't stand this. I've got to get up and...". And you just sit there.

You don't react to it. Or maybe you become interested in obsession itself. What is obsession? How do I do that? What is the payoff for obsessing? Pretty soon you lose interest in that. You become bored with it because it's not making you <u>do</u> anything. Then, maybe you turn your attention to boredom. What is boredom? How do I do that? What is the payoff for being bored? And you just sit there.

Eventually, it all begins to quiet down.

In the same way, when something happens in life you no longer believe that you have to react to it. You've sat still through so many "I can't stand thises," "emergencies," and "life and death issues," you no longer believe them. In not reacting, the very energy, the karmically conditioned force that is behind them, begins to have to feed on itself. It's no longer feeding on you because you're no longer participating in it. It has no fuel. And, eventually, it burns itself up. It simply burns itself away.

Unconditional Love

STUDENT: Yesterday I was thinking that if I'm going to learn to love myself, I need to learn to love myself just the way I am. It occurred to me that even being overweight, I need to be thankful for this opportunity to love myself. It comforts me to think I might be this way for a reason and that reason might be to learn to love myself.

GUIDE: Yes. Even if you lost weight and had a "perfect body," but had not learned to love yourself, where would you be?

STUDENT: I would still be trying to improve myself, to fix the things that I think are wrong.

GUIDE: And all you would have done is to become acceptable enough that you can love yourself conditionally, which is where we all are. As long as you do it right, look a

certain way, act the way you should, and
accomplish certain things you'll be lovable.

But can you be lovable
not meeting the standards?

Can you love this person who does not meet
the standards that you were taught must be
met before you can be lovable?

Can you stop trying to change into who you
should be and who you wish you were long
enough to find out who you really are?

You will never improve yourself enough to
meet the standards. Self-hate will see to
that.

But the moment you love yourself
unconditionally, you are completely changed.

Not wanting to be how you are is one of the most significant aspects of self-hate.

We have been taught to believe that it's not okay to feel what we feel or think what we think or have the experiences we have. As children, people didn't like us when we did that and they tried to change us. We've internalized that, and we've taken on that system ourselves. So now we're trying to change everything we don't approve of.

In acceptance, we don't want to change those things about ourselves. It's only in non-acceptance that we hope acceptance will mean they change.

We can have the full range of experience that is our potential,
and we can enjoy it all.

If we move through and beyond that conditioning to change, then everything is available to us. For example, if you're miserable, there's nothing really wrong with that, but if you're hating being miserable, then it's hell. If you're miserable and not hating it, you'll probably move through it pretty quickly.

Experiences do move along quickly when we're present and not resisting. It's when we stop being present and get stuck in something that we can drag it out forever.

We are never going to "get" something—
a philosophy,
a formula,
a fixed point of view—
that will make us forever different.

There is no secret that will fix you.
(Remember, there is nothing wrong with you.)

This is a lifelong process. If you decide to learn to care for yourself, to live your life in compassion, you will be required to practice that until you die.

An internal relationship must be worked on and maintained just like an external relationship.

And that's good news! When you fall in love with someone you don't say, "Oh, no, how long am I going to have to love this person?" When we're in love, we love to love that person, and we hope it will last forever.

When you're not letting self-hate hate you, you won't:

be chronically late,
be chronically early,
procrastinate,
work compulsively,
abuse substances,
deprive yourself,
depress your feelings,
try to be perfect,
worry too much,
worry about worrying too much,
depend on others' approval,
believe The Judge,
reject The Judge,
punish yourself,
overindulge yourself,
pass up opportunities,
be afraid of yourself,
try to improve,
try to improve others—
Add your own:

We are responsible
for being
the person we've always wanted
to find.

We must become our own best friend.
We must learn
to give to ourselves
and
receive from ourselves
unconditional love and acceptance.

It is not
selfish.
It is the first
GIANT STEP
toward
selflessness.

We call people selfish
                    when they WILL NOT give.
                        But they CANNOT give
                        what they DO NOT have.

It's like asking a starving child
                        to share her food,
and then making her feel guilty
                        for not wanting to.

When we have enough
we are eager to share.*

*What we <u>have</u> and what we are able to <u>receive</u> are two very different things.

Those who feel
completely loved
are not selfish,
they are loving.

Nothing to Do

What we're seeing here is how the layers of self-hate keep us from experiencing our intrinsic, inherent enlightenment. It's simply a matter of realizing what already is. It's not necessary for us to DO anything. What we're seeking is available to us when we stop DOING everything else.

We don't have to change.
We don't have to fix ourselves.
We don't have to improve.
We don't have to do it right.

It doesn't have anything to do with that. That's what we focus on instead of simply being here. That's why self-hate's beatings are so important to us. They are probably the single most effective method of avoiding awakening. That's why we have so much resistance to acceptance, because in acceptance there is nothing to do.

We don't need to DO anything.

To sit still
in compassionate acceptance
is all that is required.

There is a small child inside each of us who
was taught to believe that bad things
happen, or will happen, because s/he is bad.

As adults, when we become aware of this
child, we are saddened and we feel the child's
sadness. We are conditioned to try to STOP
the sadness, to move away from the
experience.

The child doesn't need for us to do that.
S/He needs to know, deep down inside, that
it is all right to be having that experience.
The child needs complete acceptance for
however s/he is in each moment. And we,
as adults, do too. That's what we didn't get
when we were little—acceptance for
however we are in whatever moment.

The only response is compassion. Trying to
STOP, FIX or CHANGE is part of the self-
hating process. Just stay with the
experience and

REALLY GET IT

that this is <u>sad</u>,
it's not wrong,
it's just hard,

it's hard to be a being.

How can we not feel compassion?

Of course, self-hate will jump right in there
and say, "Enough of this sadness. Let's DO
something about it."

That DO-ality will flip us right back into the
bottom of the pot. I imagine a big stew pot
of self-hate, and you just about crawl up to
the top of the pot when you run into
something that flips you right back in.

Usually this "something" is: trying to change what you are experiencing. Criticizing yourself, judging somebody else, thinking you need to change something, fix something, DO something—and you are right back in the bottom of the pot of self-hate

again.

Gratitude

If you find it difficult to catch the subtler self-hating processes at work, it can be helpful to sit in meditation. One of the ways we can see self-hate in a meditation practice goes
something like this:

You're sitting there, just breathing, paying attention, quiet, still.

You begin to notice that even though all you are doing is sitting silently and breathing, something is constantly scanning, trying to find just the thing that will
    pull you away
            from the stillness.

It might say things like:

This continues until something hooks you and your attention wanders. Soon you realize you have been daydreaming/fantasizing/worrying/problem solving, and you bring your attention back to the breath.

Again your attention wanders. You realize it and come back to the breath. It's important to remember not to waste time and energy believing the voices that will beat you up for having wandered. Just sit quietly in gratitude for having returned.

Self-Hate's Greatest Talent

Self-hate's greatest talent is self-maintenance. It carries on a thorough, aggressive, sometimes loud, sometimes quiet, often subtle campaign to keep us in its grip.

It would justify itself by claiming that it enables us to survive. That is a delusion.

We do not need to allow self-hate to beat,
punish,
discipline,
chastise,
berate,
and belittle us...

and we never did!

If we can ever become aware and willing enough to break the internal battering cycle and NOT ALLOW THE BEATING, we can begin to see how this is so. It takes courage

and patience and faith in our inherent
goodness.

PAINFUL THINGS COME UP
NOT TO RUIN OUR LIVES,
NOT TO MAKE US MISERABLE,
NOT TO SPOIL OUR GOOD TIME,
THEY COME UP
TO BE HEALED,
TO BE EMBRACED IN
COMPASSION.

We often wish our childhood survival system
would just go away, but once we have
embraced it, once we've realized how much
it has done for us and how much we've
learned because of it, we are grateful it
kept up the clamor. And now we can be glad
for it to go!

Self-hate is getting a new car
and not taking care of it.*

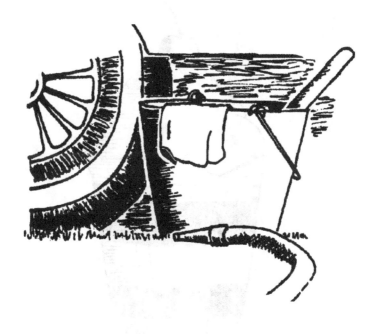

*"Not taking care of" is not taking care of yourself.

Self-hate is eating the dessert I want

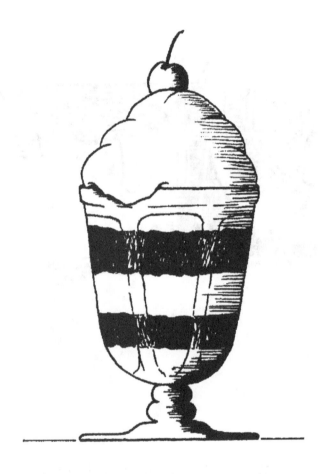

and feeling guilty the whole time.

STUDENT: Coming here today a voice was saying, "Nobody wants to hear what you have to say." Of course no one, including me, knew what I was going to say, but that doesn't stop that voice. Now that I'm here and I haven't said anything, the voice is saying, "You're not participating. You should be talking."

GUIDE: So, whatever you're doing is wrong, whatever you did was wrong, and whatever you're going to do will be wrong.

   Using a system like that to stay safe is like the cure being worse than the disease.

Self-hate is

being tortured with "It's not fair."

I look at the amount of work I do compared to my colleagues and say, "I should be making more money. It's not fair." But I'm being paid for the job I'm doing, and if I weren't being tortured with "fairness," I would not be suffering. Instead, I stay stuck in this feeling that I deserve more money, more from life than I'm getting.

To compound this self-hating mess, I'm paralyzed because I'm afraid to ask for more money, afraid to make waves, and I hate myself for being afraid.

Self-hate and Addiction

Self-hate coping behaviors
make you feel better and
make you feel worse
at the same time.

All major addictions are like this.

Self-hate is
the ultimate addiction.

GUIDE: Self-hate is an addiction and a lot of self-hate is accomplished through other addictions.

I was talking to someone last night who had been sober for four and a half years and had gone out and had a drink. I told her that when she's no longer in the grip of self-hate, she won't need to do that. When you're free of self-hate, you don't want to mistreat yourself. It's as simple as that.

With an addiction like alcohol, there has to be a time when you sit at the kitchen table with a bottle in front of you, and you sit there until you know you're not going to drink. Like the old movie <u>High Noon</u>, you've got to go out and face the Bad Guy. You may get lucky, or you may not, but you have to go out there for the showdown or pretty soon the bad guys are going to run the town. You can't hope that self-hate is going to get tired of beating you up and go away. Like blackmail, once the extortion starts, it's going to bleed you for everything you've got and then it's going to leave you for dead. It's not going to take your last dime and then leave. This isn't just turning off the faucet, it's ripping the plumbing out.

So do you want to take a chance with a confrontation, or do you want to just die a slow, lingering death? With the first choice you have a 50/50 chance; with the second, you have none. To stay with this analogy/parable/eulogy...you actually have a much better than 50/50 chance, because as soon as you strap on your six-shooter and start walking down Main Street at high noon, the Bad Guy isn't going to show up.

STUDENT: Right. Nothing bears up under scrutiny. In fact, nothing shows up under scrutiny.

GUIDE: But if you're quaking in hiding, you'll never make it to Main Street. As FDR said, "We have nothing to fear but fear itself." We are so afraid of being afraid, we are so afraid that we will be inadequate, that we won't prove to ourselves that we're not. The one who is projecting the inadequacy—in one of our previous scenes— says things like, "You think you're going to be a runner?" It's a different situation so it's sometimes hard to see that it's coming from the same source.

But who is invested in your being afraid? In maintaining an illusion of inadequacy? Do people who love you want you to be afraid? Want you to experience yourself as inadequate, unworthy, and undeserving? No, not at all.

Once we realize that fear is a process, we can get a handle on it. And there's nothing that's going to push you into this any faster than confronting the self-hate in the way that I've described because terror will arise. Every time a hateful voice comes up and starts telling you something, you just sit on the couch and read a book, or go out and look at flowers, or take yourself out to lunch, or go to a movie.

STUDENT: Then terror arises?

GUIDE: Yes. Self-hate is terrified that you will make being kind to yourself a habit.

It comes down to this for me: None of my heroes (and all my heroes are religious types) ever says, "The important thing in the universe is to be at one with fear and inadequacy." Okay? Nobody has ever defined God as "fear and inadequacy," and then said that is what you should strive for. And so, if I'm going to hold True Nature, Buddha Nature, God as the greatest value in life and on a moment-by-moment basis choose the opposite of that, then what am I doing? This is the fundamental spiritual issue. How can I go beyond this fear in order to choose wisdom, love and compassion?

STUDENT: Yes, how does one get beyond that?

GUIDE: For me, I go back to "putting the bottle on the table." I have had times in my life of sitting on my cushion and holding on to it because that's the only way I can avoid screaming or suicide or madness as every bit of my conditioning comes up inside of me and says what it says.

St. John of the Cross talked about the dark night of the soul, and to me this is exactly what he was talking about. His image of it was God and the devil wrestling for your immortal soul. And isn't that what it feels like? And doesn't it seem, most of the time, like the devil is winning?

STUDENT: Yeah. It could even look like I'm on the devil's side!

GUIDE: Yes, and so for me— and this is where I depart from a lot of the rest of the world—I really don't believe for a minute that there is something more important than that which I am seeking. **I don't think there is anything more important!** I don't think money is more important. I don't think security is more important or a good reputation or being popular or having people like me or anything else. I don't think there is anything more important than my True Nature. So, if something is coming between me and that, I am going to sit still until it is no longer there. I am simply going to sit down and sit still and keep coming back to what I know is true until there is nothing between me and that truth. I know when that is. We all know when that is. We all know that moment of oneness with our True Nature, the peace, the joy, the comfort. We know when that's there, and we know when it's not.

It's like discord in a relationship with someone I love. I am going to turn my attention to that until that lack of harmony is gone and peace, joy and comfort are back. I don't say, "I'll look at that later." I want to look at it NOW! I don't want to look at anything else until that's resolved, and I know the resolution of it is in here (points to heart). So I'm required to sit still with it.

Self-hate is like quicksand.

Everything you do to try to get out
causes you to sink deeper.

Every place you step
to try to avoid the place you're in,
also pulls you down.

In quicksand, if you stop struggling, you will
sink more slowly.

In self-hate,
when you stop struggling (when you accept),
you are free.

Compassion, No Matter What

 STUDENT: Lately, I've been saying, "Okay, I have this need and I'm going to stand up for myself and ask for what I want." So I do it, and my worst fears come true. People don't like what I said or did. My need is rejected. Then self-hate says, "I warned you!" But voice that I haven't heard before says, "But you did it. That's the important thing this time. It doesn't matter what happened afterwards, you did it."

GUIDE: Yes, we see the self-hate patterns and we learn not to believe those voices. They aren't going to stop. They're going to continue and hit a level heretofore unimagined when you start trying to break this stuff up. When you start picking away at the foundation of egocentricity, it will use everything in the world to defend itself. We can count on that. It's when things are hardest and compassion is most needed that self-hate is strongest.

If you could have compassion for yourself when you really need it, can you imagine how the self-hate system would begin to shake and crumble? You can't have too many of those experiences without beginning to question whether all of this self-hate is accomplishing what it's saying it's intended to accomplish. That's why the answer is <u>compassion, no matter what.</u>

Now, what we say is that we can have compassion as long as it's not a Really Terrible Thing we've done. But that's when we need the compassion most!

STUDENT: So if you've really done your worst, and all the self-hate voices come up, then the compassion needs to accept even those voices?

GUIDE: When we stop seeing self-hating voices as powerful and see them as pathetic, at best, we make the recipient of compassion the suffering human being who has been so abused by those hateful voices.

Willingness Is the Key.

 STUDENT: Something that has made a difference for me in understanding acceptance is realizing that things don't have to change for me to accept them. If something is happening, all I have to do is be willing to acknowledge that, and that is accepting it. It's not as if my acceptance or non-acceptance can change whether it happens or not.

GUIDE: I can't make any of this happen, but I can show up and be available. To me, that's what sitting practice is—constantly being willing to show up and be available. It's like having your hands open to receive. There's no guarantee that you're going to get anything, but if anybody wants to give you something, you're ready.

STUDENT: I'm not consistent or disciplined about sitting, but I am consistently willing to look at things and to use the world as a mirror in which to see my projections. When I look in that mirror, I see there are parts of myself I don't like and am afraid of.

GUIDE: That's the crux of the whole thing. The basis of our practice is ending suffering, and in every moment we have the opportunity to see what in us is suffering. We can ask, "What is outside the realm of compassion? What is not healed?" and we can bring that into the healing light of compassion by simply acknowledging it, accepting it, allowing it. This is the kind of person I am. This exists in me. I feel this. I do this. I have these thoughts. I have these tendencies.

The conditioned patterns of suffering
would have us hide those
so that they continue to exist
outside of compassion.

To the degree that we find the willingness to bring them into the light of compassion they are healed.

In that way, you can have all of you instead of only those things that the voices say are acceptable. You can be, you can experience, and you can have everything just being who you are in the moment.

STUDENT: Although I know how joyful it is to have that happen, it's still terrifying to find another aspect of myself that I hadn't seen before.

GUIDE: Yes, because egocentricity sees that as death. As long as there are those awful hidden things in you, self-hate can control your behavior. When you're willing to acknowledge and accept, to let everything come into the light of day, self-hate no longer has any power over you.

If I could have compassion
(love myself)
for hating myself,

I would no longer be hating myself,
I'd be loving myself,

and nothing about me
would need to change.

The Voices: Listen, but Don't Believe

If the voices in your head are saying, for example, that you're a bad spiritual student, you're a bad meditator, you fidget, and your mind wanders, at some point you could identify that as self-hate and let go of it. But, if you start thinking what a good meditator you are, what a good spiritual person you are, how well you're going, and how much better your practice is than others', that's self-hate, too, and very difficult to let go once you are hooked.

It's helpful to develop a habit of not believing any of the voices—listen, but not believe. It's as if you are sitting around a dinner table with a group of people and they're all talking. You can listen, but you don't have to decide who is right and who is wrong, who is good and who is bad, etc. You can just have the attitude of mind of being present but not involved.

When you can have that attitude of mind, it's a big step. When you can have it within yourself, you're moving toward freedom. Because the part of you that is trying to figure out which is right and which is wrong, who is good and who is bad, etc., is the problem. That's the person who is confused and suffering. When you can just step back, there isn't anything to figure out and there's nothing to believe. There's just being fully present in the moment.

The voices take us out of the moment and make us believe there is a world other than the present. The more they can get us involved in that belief, the more we're going to believe in the illusion of ourselves as separate, and the more we're going to suffer. The less we believe, the less we are seduced. The more we're able to be in the present, the less there is someone to suffer.

Learn to Be Present.

Practice hearing the voices in your head without becoming involved and without judgment.

And take it on faith that any voice, internal or external, that is saying

SOMETHING IS WRONG WITH YOU
is not the voice
of your
Heart,
God,
True Nature.

The reason acceptance
    isn't more popular
        is that in acceptance
            there is nothing to do.

In acceptance, there is nothing "wrong" that
needs to be changed, fixed, worked on or
otherwise improved.

And the simple,
astounding,
mind-bogglingly amazing
FACT
is that as soon as you accept yourself

EXACTLY

AS

YOU

ARE,

all those "character flaws"

begin to fall away because those "flaws"
exist only in non-acceptance, in self-hate.

 GUIDE: Nothing about how you are is a problem until you resist it. The problem comes into existence with resistance.

STUDENT: But what if I want to do something that's harmful?

GUIDE: Wanting to do something and doing something are two entirely different things. There's no need to act just because you have a feeling.

STUDENT: But what if I want to act?

GUIDE: Your questions come from a belief that you are inherently bad, and that if you don't control yourself, you'll be bad. When you realize that you are goodness and let yourself live from that, being harmful—intentionally harmful—would never occur to you.

If you take the most
frightening thing in the world

and invite it in,

put your arms around it,

and sit still with it,

what is left
to be frightened by?

Self-Hate: Everyone's Doing It!

Once I catch on to how this self-hate process works, I see that it goes on all the time, everywhere.

Everyone does it.
This is just how we operate.

When I see this to be true, self-hate ceases to be a private, secret thing I do that proves I'm a bad person. I can begin to take it less personally.

At some point,
now or later,
you're going to have to risk
BEING YOU
in order to find out
who that really is.

Not the conditioned you, not the "you"
you've been taught to believe you are, who
you _really_ are.

And this perhaps will be
the scariest,
the most loving,
and the most rewarding
thing you have ever done.

If you are not becoming
kinder,
gentler,
more generous,
and loving,
you are not doing this work.

If you are feeling more
burdened,
judgmental,
and rejected,
you are doing self-hate.

What Is the Path?

We find the model on the following pages to be an accurate representation of how conditioning toward fear and self-hate keeps us from knowing our original nature.

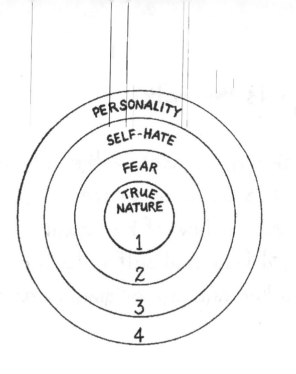

At the personality level (4), we have our coping mechanisms, our defenses, and our ways of getting by in the world. From this level, I might decide that there must be something more to life than I am getting, and that I want something more than life is offering.

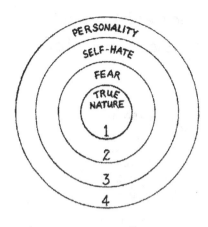

So I start working with the personality, trying to improve it, fix it, and figure it out. I decide to get a different this or that, a new mate, a new job, house, car. I pursue personal growth, get into therapy. I do all the things I think are going to turn me into the person I should be. There's nothing wrong with any of this, it just doesn't work.

Finally, all these efforts fail and I decide to take the Big Plunge and begin some kind of spiritual practice, maybe a meditation practice, something that is designed to take me beyond the personality.

I begin the long, arduous journey to the center of my being. The first thing I run into is self-hate (3). Now this is the layer that, thankfully, has been keeping the personality level from working! (Ours is a spiritual practice and does not have as its goal living a successfully egocentric life.)

So here I am at level 4 and I'm trying to become the perfect person, and level 3 is pointing out to me that it's not working. I'm

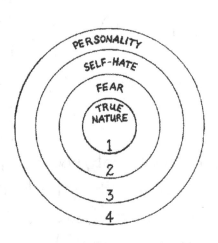

going to "improve" myself and self-hate doesn't let me. Whenever I try to make a beginning on this spiritual journey, self-hate will do anything it can to stop me and then beat me for stopping. I'm going to start meditating and self-hate stops me and beats me for stopping. I'm going to start exercising and self-hate stops me and beats me for stopping.

If I find the willingness to pay attention anyway, to struggle through the self-hating voices; if I learn to sit still through all of it and not be thrown off, the next level I encounter is fear (2).

I've made it past the distractions, I'm being compassionate with myself, and then there's this little

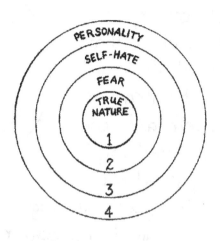

moment of silence... What do I get? Fear. Big fear. It says, "You're going to die!" And I think, "How can that be the answer? I've gone through all this and THAT'S THE ANSWER?"

So I come back to level 3, self-hate, and I see that self-hate is pretty handy because it works in both directions. I can go from fear to self-hate, and I can go from personality to self-hate. It's flexible.

I can hate myself
for being afraid,
and I can try to
fix myself so that
I'm not afraid and
I can be afraid of
the fear and I can
hate myself for
being afraid not

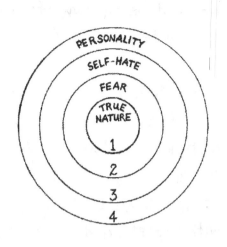

to hate myself...all designed to stop me
from getting to the center (1).

Perhaps, with patience and willingness and
experience, or plain old having suffered
enough, I eventually realize that this whole
process of going from personality to self-
hate to fear to self-hate to personality and
back again has been exactly what I needed to
learn what I needed to learn. I realize that
every step I have taken has been on the
Path. Perhaps I realize that it has all been
happening perfectly, and that True Nature
was never out of reach, always present,
always guiding me. There never was
anything wrong. I just didn't know it.

Horrible Things (and I do mean horrible)

Self-hate is invested in convincing you that you are an awful person, that deep down inside you there is some Horrible Thing. Why? Because it stays in charge that way. It can just say

BOO!

and you'll jump back and do whatever it says.

But you can call its bluff simply by saying,

"BRING OUT THE HORRIBLE THING. SHOW IT TO ME."

But self-hate can't do that.

And the more it cannot show you the Horrible Thing, the more it will dawn on you that

"MAYBE IT DOESN'T EXIST. MAYBE THERE ISN'T A HORRIBLE THING INSIDE OF ME."

Self-hate begins to scramble at this point because power is shifting away from it and shifting toward the you that is able to step back from self-hate and carry on this kind of dialogue with it, the you that can begin to stop believing there is something wrong with you, the you that is beginning to be free.

The Gift

I maintain my identity by not looking at
myself.
This system, this identity, cannot hold up
under scrutiny. Nothing can.

So... right before I begin to see myself (my
conditioned identity), ego goes on the
defensive and the voices start:

> I'm bored.
> This is stupid.
> I don't need this.
> I can't do this.
> This doesn't work for me.
> I've got too much to do.

It can sound as if we see self-hate as an
enemy, but we don't. Gandhi talked about
his political opponents as teachers, for to
have worthy opponents is a blessing. They
will force you to be the best that you are.
That's the spiritual gift
that self-hate is for us.

Regardless of what you were taught to believe, there never <u>was</u> anything <u>wrong</u> with you.

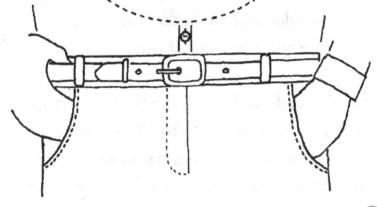

GUIDE: Okay, let's hear some self-hate. Answer this: What is wrong with you?

GROUP: Everything . . . I can't figure out what is wrong . . . I can't get it right . . . I'm never serious . . . I'm ungrateful . . . I'm critical and judgmental . . . I'm hell-bound . . . I'm angry . . . I'm never going to get what I deserve . . . I'm not a team player . . . I'm a wimp . . . I'm closed . . . I can't be trusted . . . I'm a phony . . . I'm lazy and self-indulgent . . . I'm careless . . . I'm too serious . . . I'm a coward . . . I can't get with the program . . . I'm never satisfied . . . I don't pay attention . . . I talk too much . . . I'm too slow . . . I'm a quitter . . . I don't think enough . . . I can't keep up . . . I'm not good enough . . . I'm selfish . . . I'm mean . . . I'm unfriendly . . . I'm unworthy . . . I'm unlovable . . . I'm dishonest . . . I'm proud. . . I always have to be in control . . . I can't talk right . . . I'm stupid . . . I'm out of control . . . I'm too emotional . . . I'm too sensitive . . .

GUIDE: As you were answering, I watched people grow younger and younger. You were taking a quick trip back to childhood. The voices changed, the body language changed, the energy changed. Suddenly, I was sitting in the room with a bunch of small children. They are very dear.

Self-hate uses
SELF-IMPROVEMENT
as
SELF-MAINTENANCE.

As long as
you are concerned about
improving yourself,

you'll
always have
a self to improve,
and you will always suffer.

It's No Wonder We Feel Inadequate.

Self-hate encourages you to judge and then beats you for judging.

When you judge someone else it's simply self-hate projected outward.

Then, it's all turned back on you and you get a beating for judging!

We call this,
"Heads you lose, tails you lose."

The Worst Thing that Could Happen

 STUDENT: Belief in fairness is such a setup for self-hate. "If life were fair and things were balanced the way they should be, this wouldn't be happening to me." It's easy to go from there to "I must have done something wrong." It's that old "why do bad things happen to good people?" I guess there aren't bad things and good people, just things and people.

GUIDE: And that's frightening, isn't it, because it means that we have no control. If anything can happen to us in spite of our best efforts to make things go the way we want, where does that leave egocentricity? One of ego's threats is, "If you don't do exactly as I say, something awful is going to happen to you."

If you believe this threat,
the worst thing that can happen to you
has already happened!

STUDENT: What is this "worst thing"?

GUIDE: Believing in inadequacy. Believing that you are not equal to your life. Turning away from your True Nature, your Heart, Life.

IT'S REALLY QUITE MIRACULOUS,

in the face of all our conditioned fear, to be willing even to consider sitting still with ourselves. We work and work to uncover the layers of our conditioning, and when we see what we've uncovered, our reaction is,

> "Oh, no, not that!
> I don't want to see that."

What did we think we were going to see? We must remember that this is the layer of "stuff" between the one who is seeking and that which is sought. It's what keeps me from ME. We have been taught to hate it and fear it so that we'll be too frightened and disgusted to look at it. It knows that if we ever do—if we ever get back to our unconditioned selves—

the jig is up!

Getting back to who we really are means no more self-hate, no more illusion of separateness, no more egocentricity.

That's why it's so hard and why almost no one ever does it.

Egocentricity is very powerful and very clever and very determined because it thinks it is fighting for its life.

So it looks worse and worse the deeper we go. That's why it's critical to learn to sit still and believe nothing the voices say to you. That's why it's so crucial to find compassion.

If a voice is not speaking
compassionately,
it has nothing worthwhile
to tell you.

Everything you need to know
will come to you in compassion.

Do not confuse

NICE AND POLITE

with
compassionate.

A compassionate person may be what we call nice and polite, but compassion does not try to be nice and polite.

Nice and polite
come from conditioning.

Compassion comes from the Heart
and our shared connectedness.

Fake It 'til You Make It.

STUDENT: Much of my reluctance to do certain aspects of the work of ending self-hate comes from self-hate itself. For example, if I realize I am saying bad things to myself, it seems phony to make myself be compassionate by saying something good to myself instead. But I'm finding that just making the effort is often helpful. Recently I'd been feeling crabby and not grateful, and just the mechanical act of writing "thank you" was enough to help me find the sense of gratitude. I could say that was phony and stupid, but it worked.

GUIDE: The voice saying it's phony is terrified that you'll find out how sincere you are.

STUDENT: It's okay to just pretend you like yourself, to go through the motions of embracing yourself, even if it feels false or stupid. Saint Theresa of Avila taught to go to the experience of gratitude within, and I've always assumed she meant fake it if it wasn't there. I often "act as if," and as soon as I do I feel a real change.

GUIDE: Because it's not phony. You are acting the way you really are, according to your True Nature, and that gets beneath the self-hate.

Stay with the Breath.

STUDENT: I was at a conference where we sat in meditation for an hour each morning. It was mentioned that if you hadn't sat before, you might have various physical sensations, even nausea. I had never meditated before, but I wanted to do everything right, so I sat every morning. I was pregnant at the time, and through every sitting I thought I was going to throw up. But since I knew to expect that kind of sensation, I kept sitting. I made up my mind to stick it out even if I did throw up or if I passed out.

What I learned was that I was able to get through it by staying with every single breath. The experience showed me that the internal voices weren't right. They were saying, "You can't do this, you're going to be sick." But it wasn't true, even the physical cues I was getting. That was an extremely valuable experience. Later when I was in labor, it was true again: As long as I stayed with every breath, I was all right. And that showed me where freedom is.

GUIDE: Yes. If you went to another conference and had a friend with you, say, and she was sitting those hours each day, even though she'd never sat before, you might say to her, "I hope you know what a great thing it is that you are doing. It's really hard, and you're doing it." That's the kind of thing we'll say naturally to somebody we really care about, but we don't say to ourselves. But we could. We could even go beyond telling ourselves that it's okay to have our thoughts and feelings and risk something really compassionate like. "That was really good. I'm glad you did that. You're a good person." When I make those recommendations, people often say they're afraid that if they are that kind to themselves they will become egocentric and self-indulgent. But we already are egocentric and self-indulgent! Being kind to ourselves is the way not to be egocentric and self-indulgent!

It's Okay to Feel Afraid?

 STUDENT: I've found it very helpful in meditation to tell myself that I love myself. At first it felt sort of phony and ridiculous, but I decided to keep at it, and the results have been amazing. Sometimes I've been in terrible mental states, and the idea of loving myself will come up all by itself. It's brought me to tears at times because the compassion is right there. I've practiced verbalizing "I love you" to myself, and as a result those words will just arise.

GUIDE: The fact that we see it as phony and ridiculous tells us that egocentricity is doing the judging. From a centered place, you would never see loving yourself as phony and ridiculous. Only ego would add those labels. Calling it phony is self-hate. It's ego trying to get you to believe that loving yourself is an experience that you don't know. That's why I like this process of reassuring myself that I do love myself.

An example of acceptance and lovingkindness for the self in daily life could be something like this: Let's say that I've identified that I'm afraid. I could say, "I am a brave and courageous person," but that's not going to do any good. Or I could say, "It's okay to be afraid," and begin to focus on what this fear is. "What is fear? What does it feel like? Where does it happen in my body? What do I say to myself when I'm afraid?" I might go ahead and do the thing I'm afraid of, and then I can ask, "At what point does the fear arise? How does the fear stop me from doing this thing? Can I feel the fear and do it anyway?" So, you see, there's somewhere to go with it. If it's okay to be afraid, all my options are open.

Am I afraid all the time? No. Well, when am I afraid? What exactly am I afraid of? If I'm trying to hide the fear, repress it, and not let myself know that I have it, it can become a weapon for self-hate.

Instead of being someone who is afraid of a specific thing, I get labeled by self-hate as a frightened, fearful, whining, needy, cowardly person. But if I'm just afraid of something, and that's okay, that nonjudgment is an open doorway that I can go through. The acceptance brings me back to myself. I can be still with the fear as it's happening, experience it for what it is, and allow it to be healed within that acceptance.

Fear is very dramatic.
It tells very plausible stories.
It makes strong feelings in your body.
It is the primary support of egocentricity.
It is egocentricity.

Ego is fear, and ego is everything it does to
manage,
control,
and avoid
that fear, that experience of itself.

(It says, "I'll protect you. I'll keep you
safe.")

**Ego spends enormous amounts of
time and energy
pretending to avoid itself!**

Pay attention.
Self-hate is slippery.
It will even say things to you like,

"You shouldn't believe the voices of self-hate. If you are still believing them, there really is something wrong with you!"

I am not here to become
an acceptable person.

I am here to accept
the person I am.

It May be True...

It may be true that you make sacrifices, but that doesn't make you good, it just means you make sacrifices.

It may be true that you are accepting, but that doesn't make you good, it just means you are accepting.

It may be true that you are responsible, but that doesn't make you good, it just means you are responsible.

It may be true that you meditate, but that doesn't make you good, it just means you meditate.

We label these behaviors good and then continue to do them in order to support self-hate. Perhaps <u>doing</u> in order to be good is what keeps you from realizing that you already are good.

It may be true that you gossip, but that doesn't make you bad, it just means you gossip.

It may be true that you tell lies, but that doesn't make you bad, it just means you tell lies.

It may be true that you are impatient, but that doesn't make you bad, it just means you are impatient.

It may be true that you are sarcastic, but that doesn't make you bad, it just means you are sarcastic.

We label these behaviors bad and then continue to do them in order to support self-hate. Believing that what you do determines who you are could be the real reason for continuing the behaviors.

It's a lose/lose game
with self-hate.

If I feel good
I have to pay the price
because it's not really okay to feel good.

If I feel bad
I have to pay the price
because it's not really okay to feel bad.

But I Could Make a Mistake!

STUDENT: I've heard you say that it's not possible to make mistakes. I'm having some difficulty understanding this. Would you say more about it?

GUIDE: Whatever it is that I'm doing, if I pay attention to it I'm going to learn something, and I'm going to benefit.

Look at your son, Evan, learning to walk. At what point should he have considered himself a failure and given up? All of the times he pitched over on his head or fell back on his bottom? Those were not successful from the definition of walking, yet they were not unsuccessful, either. They were just part of the process of learning to walk. If we want to wake up and end suffering (and if we are paying attention to how we cause ourselves to suffer), we want to to learn from everything that happens. For example, I am going along in life working diligently toward something, and it doesn't go the way I want it to go. If I am willing to pay attention, not getting what I want is very helpful.

"Why didn't I get what I wanted?"
"Why wasn't I in control?"
"What went wrong?"
"Who's to blame?"
"What should I have done differently?
"Maybe I should try harder."

Well, now, there's a classroom for you!
If you were to see clearly all your conditioned beliefs about getting what you want, control, wrong, blame, should, and trying, you would have a level of clarity that would make your life simple and enjoyable in a way that you cannot now even imagine. You would have a level of freedom available to you that you would never find if everything went the way you want it to for the rest of your life.

Failure, making mistakes...the person who is agonizing over "should I take that job in Hoboken," as if transportation only goes in one direction. If you take the job and that's not where you want to be, you're dooooooomed to stay there forever. It's not possible to say, "Oh, I don't like Hoboken," and leave. It becomes life and death, all or nothing.

This reminds me of early Ram Dass with questions like:

"Should I cut my hair?"
"Should I lose my virginity?"
"Should I read Meher Baba?"

For us, I suppose it would be:

"Should I read Rajneesh?"

(And, of course, the answer is RISK IT.)

But the attitude of mind that is focused on this sort of thing has already failed.

If you are afraid of making a mistake, you've already made it. You're already in as bad a place as you can be in. Everything after that is getting out.

This kind of information is not well received by self-hate because what would it beat you with if it weren't possible to fail? If there were no such thing as a mistake? If you couldn't do it wrong? And if there were nothing to beat you with, where would the control come from? What would maintain the fear? What would maintain the anxiety and the inadequacy?

And the questions that follow those are: What would maintain egocentricity? How would you know who you are? How would you know who you "should" be or what you "should" do?

It is only the illusion of a separate self (something that believes itself to be outside of life and living in other than the Now, which is the only reality) who could believe it is possible to make mistakes. Because, in fact, there isn't anything going on other than what is. It is only in some imaginary parallel universe—in which this is what did happen, but that is what could have happened—that that kind of alternative seems plausible. In this universe there is only what is. Everything else is delusion.

As far as I know, it is only when we hold the notion that something happened _this_ way, but it should have happened _that_ way that we can say, "I had _this_ experience, but _that_ is the one I was supposed to have." I don't think so.

STUDENT: From the perspective of the part of me who believes in failure, none of what you're saying makes sense, and yet, what you're saying makes sense.

GUIDE: That's why, when we look at these issues, it is very helpful to come back to center, to the present moment, to look at them because self-hate is _invested in failure_.

The payoff for failing?

AS LONG AS YOU FAIL, you have to do it again. "I don't have it quite right so I have to do it again."

STUDENT: How could that be a payoff?

GUIDE: It maintains egocentricity, my place at the center of the universe. The whole universe is hinged on "Will I succeed?"

I will say again what I have said so often. The reason acceptance, simply accepting what is, is not more popular is that in acceptance there is nothing to do. Egocentricity is doing.

And remember, self-hate/egocentricity/fear/the illusion of separation is ultimately concerned with only one thing: maintaining itself.

I suspect we focus on "learning from our mistakes" (being beaten up over them) because that keeps us from paying attention to what is happening

NOW.

Remember, as long as you are out of the moment, self-hate is in control.

Non-acceptance is always suffering, no matter what you're not accepting.

Acceptance is always freedom, no matter what you're accepting.

A Definition of Suffering

Trying to get and hold on to
that which we like,

and

trying to avoid and eliminate
that which we do not like.

Whatever is struggling
or discontented
or suffering
or afraid

is that which needs
to be accepted.

Life is very short.

We do not have time to be frightened.
We do not have the luxury of allowing fear
and hate to run our lives.

THIS IS IT!

Self-Hate and the Illusion of Control

We're tense and stress-filled, trying to control life. We tense up, hold on tightly, and feel that we're making something happen (what we want), or keeping something from happening (what we don't want). If, in fact, by tensing up we could control life, we'd be foolish not to. However, what we know is that being tense, being filled with stress, does <u>not</u> enable us to control life.

Aren't we then quite foolish to maintain the tension? Because with this tense/no control situation, we have two problems:
1. tension/stress and
2. no control over life.

In a no tension/no control situation, we would have only one problem:
no control over life

which can be experienced
as frightening or freedom.

We have no control but we think we **should**
have. Letting go of the illusion of control
will not make you more vulnerable, it will
make you more relaxed, peaceful, open,
receptive, joyful, calm.

Children have no control and don't
think they should have.

"Yes, but look what happens to kids!"

Life is life with or without the illusion
of control. Children feel the pain of life.
Pain and suffering are not the same thing.

**Suffering happens when we are taught
to believe that what is happening to us
is wrong and a mistake and we should
have prevented it.**

We **learn** to think of life as reward and
punishment.
-- If I'm good, good things happen to me. I
get what I want. ("Eat your peas then you
can have pie.")

-- If I'm bad, bad things happen to me. I don't get what I want, and things will be withheld from me. ("You didn't do your homework. No screens for you tonight.")

We learn to believe that if we exert enough control, if we are how we "should" be, we can have only the good things in life and keep "bad" things from happening. We learn to believe that what happens to us is the result of how we are. Life punishes us when we're bad and rewards us when we're good.

By the time we're adults we are firmly entrenched in "Things are going my way. That means I'm a good person." Or "I'm not getting what I want. I'm being punished for being bad."

This is what's going on in a nutshell: We have learned to believe that self-hate— that relentless onslaught of judgment, criticism, and blame—prevents us from being cruel, exploitative, selfish, and indulgent, and that without being constantly watched and controlled we will be hateful and harmful. It's a lie!

Self-hate won't prevent
the abuse of little children
who are currently in little bodies,
and it won't prevent the abuse
of little children who are currently
in big bodies (such as your own).

The only way
we are ever going to stop abuse
in all its forms
is by ceasing to believe
that punishing people
makes them good.

You cannot be nonviolent if there is any part of yourself that you are in opposition to.

You are not truly giving if there is any part of yourself to which you will not extend compassion.

Your love will always be conditional as long as you are excluding any part of yourself from it.

Suffering cannot be healed through self-hate. Only through compassionate acceptance can suffering be healed.

If we accept, if we open ourselves, life will transform us.

If we resist, if we try to run away, pain and suffering are reinforced, and we deepen the conditioning that causes us to suffer.

When we embrace,
        the pain
                wears the suffering
                        away...

 If we can be willing and patient, life will work its magic on us.

Little by little, all that is not compassion will be stripped away, burned away from us.

The pain and suffering of holding on to our beliefs and fears will become so great that we will let go. And each time we let go, we find peace, relief, ease, and a growing sense of gratitude and compassion.

Meditation Will Take Care of It.

STUDENT: I wake up in the night afraid of dying. I don't know what to do.

GUIDE: Meditating will take care of it for you. You will be able to experience directly what you are labeling fear. What is fear actually? "Well, I'm afraid I'm going to die." You are going to die, that's true. Are you dying in this moment? Not so that it shows. Is it an experience you're having or is it an idea you're holding on to? What would that sensation be without those beliefs, those labels, without that conditioning?

You wake up, everything is fine. A thought comes through, the fear follows it, then the voices kick in, and you're off to the races. **There was nothing going on before that.** How did you get there? What happened?

STUDENT: There were times when I would stay awake all night.

GUIDE: Believing every bit of what the voices in your head were saying, right? So, you begin to see how that kind of process has served a purpose in your life. Now, the purpose may be no more complex than it perpetuates self-hate. It keeps you down. It keeps you terrified. It keeps you stuck. It keeps you "safe". You start to take a risk, you feel the icy hand around the spine at 3.00 a.m., you knock off that risk-taking. Just get back to that safe place. Start doing all of those behaviors that make egocentricity feel in control and feel safe. Narrow that world down. Do what you're supposed to do. Be beaten mercilessly and then maybe you'll be all right.

Through practicing here at the Zen Center and through paying attention in your meditation, you begin to suspect that what's really going on is a process that has nothing to do with what you think is going on. You begin to see that there are certain times when these patterns happen. You begin to notice that they are, in fact, patterns.

You're no longer believing them. You're
bringing it back closer and closer to the
sensation that's actually triggering it. And
you realize that there is no such thing as
fear.

Beginning to wake up.
Beginning not to take it personally.
Beginning to see
that life isn't anyone's "fault."

It just is
and you just are,
and it's all just fine.

Going Out, Getting Miserable, Coming Back

To me, the psychological work we do is wonderfully helpful, but it's useless without sitting practice. However, sitting practice is not useless without the psychological aspect. You could just sit down and face a wall and eventually you would understand all of this. It's all available without having any intellectual understanding of it. However, the two together are a really solid program for ending suffering. But most people want to have *only* an intellectual understanding and then make that work for them. That's like having an intellectual understanding of riding a bicycle. It's great when you're sitting in the living room with a book reading about it, but when you are flying down a hill, it doesn't help. The only thing that's helpful is doing it, practicing.

In our sitting practice, we go to that place of inherent goodness, we find that deep sense of well-being within ourselves, and we become friends with that. We go there, and we see that being there is wonderful. For the periods of time that we're there, all the problems fall away, everything falls into place. And then we leave that and go get caught up in something. And we come back.

That's why I talk about, rather than taking spiritual practice into daily life, we bring daily life into spiritual practice. We're creating a circle of compassion, and we keep bringing the events of life into it. If I am upset about something, I bring it into that still, peaceful place and it just resolves itself. Then I get caught up again, my mind takes off, I go into conditioning, and I'm miserable. Then I come back. I practice coming back here (indicating center), going out, getting miserable, coming back here.

Eventually, I get to the point where when I look at being here in the place of compassion or out there caught up in self-hate, there's just no question about it. I don't want to be out there caught up in self-hate.

It's not that I'm pushing that away; it's not that I'm saying I'm a bad person for doing that. It's just that I look at it, I realize what's going on, and I prefer to come back here.

Who's Afraid of Me? I'm Afraid of Me!

The benefit of working to see and let go of self-hate is that you cease to be afraid of yourself, and you find a greater willingness to sit down and be still with whatever is there inside you. When you stop believing

the voices of self-hate, you will notice a curious thing— emptiness, a hole inside yourself. Instead of distracting yourself and trying to fill it up, if you become curious about how to sit down and be with the emptiness, it is a very wonderful thing.

When we try to fill up that hole with distractions, we feel empty. That emptiness is full of suffering; it's a narrow, closed experience. The other emptiness is an open, spacious feeling, and yes, ego resists because ego doesn't exist there. Getting used to that spaciousness is a wonderful experience.

In the present,
we can embrace the past
and free the future.

If the future
is not freed to be the present it is,
our present will always
be lived in the past.

 GUIDE: I asked people if they had had a pleasant evening, and many indicated that they had not. So could we hear from some of the victims of post self-hate workshop self-hate?

STUDENT: When I left the workshop, I felt a sense of gratitude. "Here's the road to freedom and I had forgotten. It's very helpful to be reminded." Then I watched self-hate use that information against me.

This was the situation. Part of me is very indecisive. In trying to decide whether I should spend the evening doing A or B, she became totally flustered and just wanted someone to tell her what to do. Then a self-hate voice said, "That's duality. The answer is not to do it." And then another judging voice said, "What you need is compassion, and you're not giving it to yourself." So self-hate took everything I learned yesterday and plugged it into the self-hating system.

I was left with this indecisive person who was suffering horribly, and then I heard another voice say, "You're just maintaining self-hate." Afterwards, I could see that it was that voice that was maintaining self-hate; the person who was miserable was just miserable. And I wasn't doing anything to help her because I was accusing her of doing it wrong.

Finally I cried and that seemed to release something. But I can see why people would stop paying attention. You start to see all this stuff, and it would be easy to decide that it's just too much.

GUIDE: And who would decide that it's "just too much" except self-hate? Self-hate doesn't decide it's "too much" when it's beating you up—only when you have become aware and are seeing what it is doing to you does it say "too much." Doesn't that timing make you a little suspicious?

If it's really too much, then stop allowing beatings for being who you are. Isn't that where the misery comes in? SO

WHAT if you have trouble making a decision? SO WHAT if you want someone to tell you what to do? SO WHAT if it's duality? SO WHAT if you're maintaining egocentricity? Would any of it be a problem if you hadn't been taught to believe that how you are is wrong? Will anybody die or have something awful happen to them as a result of how you are? No. So how do we justify all this violence? Someone has a hard time deciding between A and B. Should we kill her? Is she not fit to live? Or is it enough that she is simply beaten until she doesn't care if she lives? Can you see how insane this system is? How could violence and hatred improve anything? I would encourage you to risk the horrors of indecision and compassion.

I don't see grownups in this. I just see little children, because that's how most of us feel inside. I picture this child who doesn't know whether she wants the red bucket or the blue bucket. The truth is, she wants them both. They're both really pretty and she likes them equally, and she can't make up her mind. What she doesn't know is that in this world, you only get one because getting both makes you selfish.

What's going to help her out here? How about if we start yelling at her about making up her mind? About how if she doesn't decide soon, she's not going to get either one? Would it help if our voices sound angry and our faces are red and we grab her by the arm and shake her? No. And yet how many children are "taught" in that manner?

Not knowing whether you want A or B, red or blue, does not make you a bad person. Those things have nothing to do with each other. But isn't it hard to see that? We've been taught that everything in life makes you either a good person or a bad person. But it's not true, and it never was.

All of life's conflicts are between
letting go
or
holding on,

opening into the present
or
clinging to the past,

expansion
or
contraction.

The Path of Patient Effort

Once upon a time there was a student who came faithfully to Zen retreats, but always in the grips of the belief that she was a Bad Meditator. At every retreat she agonized about this, and every time she said the same things: "I can't meditate. I sit on the cushion and I think about things, I daydream, I write books, I fidget. I just can't do this." And the teachers would say, "That's all right. Just keep showing up. Sit there. Pay attention when you can." Retreat after retreat, the same thing went on.

After five years, suddenly the Good Meditator showed up at a retreat. There was nothing to fight against any longer, and the part of the student who wanted more than anything to meditate was finally able to come to a retreat. Now, the Good Meditator was the one who had been bringing the student to every retreat all along, and taking whatever meditation time it could get. Self-hate told her endlessly

what a bad meditator she was. But the
Good Meditator patiently stayed with it, and
finally the student was able to see that part
of herself. Moral of the story: No matter
what anybody says, don't give up on yourself.

Acceptance is the path to creativity,
in fact,
it _is_ creativity.

Until you accept, nothing new can be;
you will have only the past.

If you want a new world,
accept the world as it is.

If you want a
wholly new world,
accept it wholly.

SAY

YES

TO LIFE

When the Buddha wanted to find out how suffering happened and how to end it, and discovered that no one could tell him, his response was to find out for himself.

It is possible for each of us to do this, although almost none of us want to.

Almost Nobody Wants to Grow Up.

We think it's too hard. We would rather focus on what's wrong with us and why we can't do anything about it.

We don't want to take care of ourselves because that means giving up the wish to be taken care of by someone else.

"I want my mother to do it. She should have done it but she didn't. I'm going to stay stuck right here until..."

Until what? Until she does it? But she can't do it. And she never could.

Again, we need to consider this: If we can't do it, how could somebody else have done it? "Well I could do it now if she had done it then."

No.

That's a scam run by egocentricity designed to keep you stuck.

We look for things that were done to us because that makes us The Victim. When we are The Victim, things are not our fault and we don't have to take responsibility. We can point to all these reasons that we are how we are.

We can also say, yes, this did happen to me, and my parents did it to me because their parents did it to them, and so on down the line. And if I can't stop doing it to myself, how can I expect them to have stopped doing it? They weren't aware any of this existed. They were just being good parents in the same way they were parented.

ALMOST NOBODY WANTS TO GROW UP.

Taking responsibility
is not
taking blame.

It's not your fault.
It's not someone else's fault.
It's not anyone's fault.

"FAULT" MISSES THE POINT.

This is how it is.
This is your best opportunity to turn it
around.*

*There will always be future opportunities, but why not use
this one?

Paraphrase of an old Zen story:

One hot summer afternoon the monastery cook, an elderly monk, was spreading mushrooms on a mat to dry in the sun. A young monk saw him and asked, "Why is an old man like you doing such hard work in the heat of the day?" The old monk replied, "If not me, who? If not now, when?"

Paraphrase of another old Zen story:

A woman went to a Zen monastery. She was so thrilled to be there—such a holy place, a place of enlightenment.

The first sitting period, she walked mindfully up the steps of the meditation hall. As she was preparing to bow deeply before entering, she noticed a shocking thing. There, at the top of the steps, was a bucket of filthy wash water with a mop protruding from the murky depths. "That's awful!" she exclaimed, truly horrified, and went in to meditate.

The next morning the bucket was still there.

"That's disgusting," she muttered, "this is Zen?" and went in to meditate.

The next morning, the same bucket. She exclaimed, "I can't believe this! This is ridiculous. Someone should do something about this," and went in to meditate.

The fourth morning, there was the bucket, hardly improved by the days of neglect.

The woman looked at the bucket and thought, "I'm someone," and took it away and cleaned it.

People 40, 50, 60 years old
are waiting for their parents
to parent them.

"I don't want to have to love myself. I want
my mother to love me. I want my father to
give me what I need."

The odds are very good
that's not going to happen.

If your parents could love you the way you
want to be loved,
             it would have happened already.

Only you
know how you want and need to be loved.

Only you
can love you the way you want and need to
be loved.

If you can't or won't give yourself what you need, how do you suppose someone else, who isn't nearly so motivated, who, in fact, is looking to get it for themselves (possibly from you!) is going to provide it for you?

ALMOST NOBODY WANTS TO GROW UP.

You can have it all.

Living from compassion for ourselves
gives us each
the loving parent
we've always wanted.

GUIDE: I used to think I was going to find within myself a grownup to parent my child. I've discovered that it's really a case of finding the child who can care for the grownup! The secret is this. The adult is the abused product of society's conditioning, while the child, who was (thank goodness) abandoned so that this person could survive, is still here inside, whole and complete and original.

What we are doing in awareness practice is experiencing that who we are is not the self-hating social conditioning. Who we are is the conscious compassionate awareness that is our essential nature. As we learn to live more from essence, we grow to realize that it is our opportunity, our joy, and our delight to embrace into unconditional love and acceptance all that suffers.

You have to take responsibility for living
TODAY
the life you want to live.

WHAT I WANT IN MY LIFE	CHECK(✔) ONE		
	YES	NO	MAYBE
ACCEPTANCE			
REJECTION			
COMPASSION			
JUDGMENT			
CLARITY			
SHOULDS			
FREEDOM			
RESISTANCE			
MASTERY			
OTHER			

The only difference between the life you
are living and the life you want to live is the
feeling of being appreciated, loved, and
accepted. Unconditionally.

So...
give it to yourself RIGHT NOW!
                THIS MINUTE!
                DON'T WAIT!

Not when you've changed. Not when you're
in a better mood. Not when you've earned
it. RIGHT NOW! You could start with
appreciating yourself for reading this book,
for caring, for being willing, for opening your
heart.

There is nothing in life
that could happen to you
that is worse than living in fear and self-
hate.

And the great sadness
is that living in fear and self-hate
won't keep what you fear and hate
from happening to you.

We cling to our belief that there is
something wrong

There is something
wrong with this
universe, and
I need to fix it.

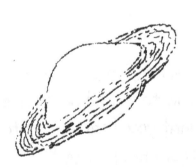

because that's how we maintain our position
at the center of the universe.

Self-Hate Doesn't Work (or does it?)

 GUIDE: Getting beaten up over something is a really good scam because while I'm over here being beaten (once again I've eaten something I shouldn't eat), I'm really over here working at improving my character (if I could just handle this compulsive eating, then I would be the person I should be), conveniently not noticing that over there I'm getting set up to collude with self-hate to allow it to punish me when I don't meet the standard (I'm so stressed out I need a treat, maybe a banana split or maybe just an iced mocha latte with extra whipped cream...). So, it works in two ways.

Submitting to self-hate's punishment makes me feel that I am doing the best I can do to become the person I should be. And even though I'm "failing" to be the person I should be, I get rewarded because I try so hard and I get punished so much.

STUDENT: It's difficult to see, until it's been pointed out several million times, that this way of improving my character, which I've been diligently doing all my life, doesn't have the desired effect.

GUIDE: In fact, it has the opposite effect, which is why we do it. For example, it's hard for people like us to feel like victims, but if I don't feel like a victim, how can I justify my privileged position in life? I can't, and so the only way I can feel like a victim is to victimize myself. I work so hard and I try so hard and I allow self-hate to punish me constantly and, my god, I need a trip to Nepal to try to get some relief, to find some meaning in this life, you know? Or I need a new car because I am victimized by this hideous commute.

STUDENT: I have learned so deeply that if I say no to self-hate's punishment, I'm not a good person, and that those two things are equal. The more I'm punished for doing bad stuff, the better, more virtuous person I am.

GUIDE: Of course, as soon as we take a look at it, we realize it never worked and it still doesn't work and, in fact, we have no evidence that it ever worked on anybody. It didn't work on us when we were kids, and it hasn't worked on us since we've been adults. It doesn't work on any kids we know. It doesn't work. Why do we continue to do it then?

STUDENT: Because it does work in a superficial way. I can be beaten up for doing something bad and let it scare me enough that I won't do that bad thing again. So on this level, you can say that it does work.

GUIDE: I think it does work, but not in the way we like to pretend it does. It works in that it enables me to do anything I want to do because I have to make up to myself for all the punishment I've received in life. It

goes like this: I'm punished in ways that
reinforce my identity and then talked into
indulging myself in ways that maintain my
identity. It's a balancing act in which ego will
be hard on me in these ways so that I can
be talked into indulging myself in these ways.

I'm punished for...
not working hard enough
being afraid
wanting to be in control
having too little ambition
being a perfectionist

which allows me to indulge...
blaming others
feeling guilty
"Whatever. I don't care!"
shirking responsibility
rationalizing dishonesty to get ahead

Most of us are pretty good at
balancing these two. The result:
maintenance of identity. Ego wins and ego
wins.

Nothing to Do, No One to Do It

When you are in the present moment,
there is no you that is separate and alone,
no identification with egocentricity.

> Self-hate is designed
> to make sure that doesn't
> happen.

Self-hate will pull you out of the experience
of the present moment in order to get you
to focus on "What's wrong? What did I do?"
It's that self-conscious questioning and
analysis that brings you out of the present
moment, either into the past...

"How should I have been instead of how I
was?"

or into the future...

"What should I do about it?"

It doesn't matter what happened

THEN.

All that matters is what happens

The best reason to look at self-hate is that self-hate gets in the way of being able to do spiritual practice.

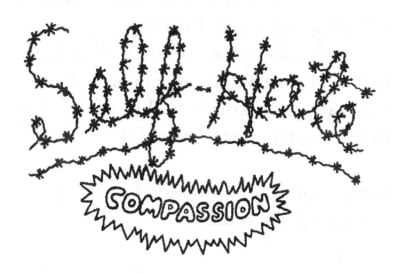

It gets in the way of finding that place of deep compassion within ourselves that is the largest part of spiritual practice.

Sitting Still, Sitting With

 When I first came to a spiritual practice, I thought I would learn to sit and all my conditioning, my suffering, and my past would just go away and I would simply be centered. Now I see that sitting means sitting <u>with</u> all of that, allowing it to be exactly as it is, not needing to do something about any of it.

Every time I try to fix myself,
I compound the problem.

When the conditioning can just come up and pass away, it loses power, it loses momentum.

In this way, sitting still with it
dissolves it,
burns it away,
strips it away.

What's Really Going On

This is why meditation, paying attention, awareness, and long retreats are helpful:

You are sitting still.
You are watching, watching, watching. After several days, the world sort of goes away. The system cannot maintain the same connections because it tends to start focusing on whatever is going on around you, and there's not much going on. So everything starts slowing down, everything starts simplifying. There's really nothing to do except turn your attention inward...

Then you begin to see what the programming is really like. You begin to hear more clearly the

things you are being told, things you couldn't hear until everything became very quiet.

The watching creates spaciousness. Your attention focuses.

It's like having a microscope. Now you can begin to see what's really going on.

We Have A Choice.

We can live our lives trying to conform to some nebulous standard, or

we can live our lives seeing how everything works.

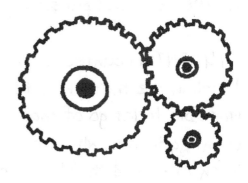

When we step back and look at it that way, it is obvious that

the attitude of fascination
is the only intelligent one to bring to anything.

A Useful Pursuit

 STUDENT: When I first started sitting in meditation, I figured out how many breaths it would take until I could get up again.

GUIDE: A useful pursuit.

STUDENT: I counted the number of breaths I took in the thirty-minute meditation. I was able to let go of that and started counting to ten, which you taught me to do. Then I realized that had become a crutch. I would figure out how many sets of ten it would take to get through. When I couldn't stand it anymore, I'd think, "I'll breathe five more sets of ten, and we'll be through." But I realized that was not helpful either and judged myself saying, "You're doing this wrong." So I made a rule that I couldn't count to ten. And then I thought, "If the choice is either count from one to ten or not sit at all, I'm going to count from one to ten."

GUIDE: Counting from 1 to 10 is not going to make me enlightened, but not counting from 1 to 10 is not going to make me enlightened either.

STUDENT: Ego says, "This is so stupid. This is a waste of time." And yet my experience is not that at all.

GUIDE: Exactly. If ego were to say, "I don't want to meditate anymore, I'm terrified, I'm afraid I'm going to die," it would be clear to us. But instead it says, "This is stupid. How long have I been doing this? Sitting here counting 1, 2, 3, 4..."

And it's very convincing. So then to be able to come back to center enough to say, "If somebody in me thinks this is boring and stupid, but somebody else in me wants to do it, why not let her do it?" To learn how to sit still when we hate what's going on, to learn to sit still when it's really hard is very good. There's nothing to do but let go of the idea that you have any control. Breathe in, breathe out, breathe in, breathe out.

Are you going to feel better? No. Are you going to get everything that you want? No. But there's no alternative—what is, is. You can say, "Okay, I'll just be all right with this," giving up all hope, all expectation, all illusion that you can affect anything. Breathe in. Breathe out. It's not a bad deal. Learning to sit still when there is nothing that you can do about what you're experiencing is incredibly valuable.

Ego will say, "Sitting used to be fun. I used to love to sit. It was easy to sit. I wanted to sit. I would go to retreats so I could sit a lot. Now I hate it. I don't want to be having this experience of sitting. I want to feel like I felt before." But you don't. Can you learn to love the experience that you're having? To open yourself completely to the experience of hating what's going on? Not repressing, not denying, just letting go completely into that experience and finding out what that's like?

Can you get a feel for what I'm saying? Let yourself hate it. Let yourself be angry. Let yourself have a fit. It would be good for you. It would be very therapeutic for you.

STUDENT: What I saw as you were talking is that I have this idea of how sitting is supposed to be.

GUIDE: Exactly, but how sitting is, is how sitting is. And how it is for you right now is miserable. So you get to experience feeling miserable. And if all you're being is miserable, miserable is not bad. It's only when you're miserable and hating miserable that it's really hell.

There's nothing more important than compassion. Anything other than compassion is designed to pull us off center. Everything other than compassion is ego. Don't fall for it. You can embrace it all in compassion, just like you would a mischievous child. But if there is judgment it is coming from ego. From center, from compassion, there is no judgment. There is no element of wrong or bad. You don't have to be fooled any longer. Ego will be the one who's saying, "Well, yeah, but that isn't a judgment. That's just clarity of perception. I'm actually centered and I can see that from a centered place, it's really not good to be that way." WRONG.

STUDENT: It seems very helpful to have an external person saying, "Do you see how you're looking from ego here?" Is the idea to eventually have that kind of perspective internally?

GUIDE: Absolutely. What you're learning to do through this practice is see the place from which the Guide looks. When you're with the Guide you can see that very clearly. You move in and out of that place, right? And you're finding that place inside of you. And eventually that will become your—and this has to be in quotes—"identity." You will live from that place. You will be pulled off occasionally into ego, but you will live from there.

When you simply watch the next movement
of the mind,

and the next,

and the next,

the whole mass of conditioning you've been
taught to believe begins

to

fall

away.

Miracles

It is a miracle:

to want to sit in meditation,

to sit in meditation and have your attention
wander and then come back to the breath,

to get your head above water (or out of the
stew pot) for any length of time,

to have even a glimmer of how it all works,

to have the willingness to practice at all.

Jesus said,

"You must become as little children."

He was talking about having as our primary identity the innocent Heart, not the conditioned mind.

From the innocent, compassionate Heart it is clear that life just happens. We don't need to take it personally. We are not being punished, and neither are we being rewarded. It is only when we are identified with our socialized, conditioned minds that we have difficulty with any of it.

STUDENT: I've been thinking about the line from St. John, "Perfect love casts out fear." To me, that means going back to the breath at any moment because there is the perfect compassion that will cast out fear. How else can we challenge that subtle kind of fear?

GUIDE: Going back to the breath means letting go beliefs, and without beliefs, you cannot be afraid.

STUDENT: It's really hard to put love in the place of fear, but just going back to the breath isn't hard at all—there's nothing to do but breathe.

GUIDE: Exactly. Trying to make love be there is _doing_ something. Dropping everything and coming back to the breath is not doing anything. But in that place is the unconditional love you are seeking.

STUDENT: So if we want to have any kind of life that is moving toward freedom, we have to be continually returning to the breath.

GUIDE: Yes. That is the direction of finding compassion. It's important to see that compassion is not something we do. In fact, when you drop everything and come back to the breath, there's nothing going on, is there? Afterwards, we can say that it was peaceful or joyful or it felt like unconditional love, but when we're just with the breath, nothing is there. We want to make it something so we can have a subject-object relationship with it. But in the experience, there is literally nothing going on. There's no self-hate, no problem in the future, no problem in the past. We can accustom ourselves to being in that place. It becomes more and more familiar, and there is a sense of deeper identity—the Identity that all beings share.

We practice coming back to that place again and again and again. And every time, everything falls away. Then we wander off into all this stuff again, then we drop it and come back to the breath. We practice doing that with little things so we can experience that it's all right. So, I'm thinking about something, and I realize I'm just thinking so I drop the thought and come back to my breath. And nothing is lost. I'm not repressing anything. I'm not avoiding anything. I'm simply dropping that ego identity maintenance system and coming back to the moment. As I learn that there's no danger in this process, no fear, no loss, I can practice it with bigger things until, one day, in the middle of something big and scary, I can drop it and come back to the breath. The process is exactly the same as for little things. I no longer believe that because it's a big scary thing it's more real. I know the answer is to drop it and come back to the breath.

Egocentricity's job is to counter that by insisting that if I drop it and go back to the breath, I will die. That's why I have to practice dropping every different thing that comes up a million times. I practice and practice and practice, and when that voice comes up saying I'm going to die if I don't do such and such, my response is, "I haven't died yet. How many times have you told me I was going to die and I haven't? Your credibility is slipping."

STUDENT: It took me a long time to see that "I'm going to die" is not necessarily a verbal message. For me, it's more a physical sensation, and also emotional upheaval, which I had to see time after time to realize that the underlying message was that I would die.

GUIDE: "I can't stand it" is another form it can take.

STUDENT: And still that space between the "I" dropping it and going back to the breath involves an incredible leap of faith.

On the Path

Doing this work alone is difficult though certainly not impossible. At livingcompassion.org you will find many ways to support yourself in keeping a perspective of disidentification that self-hate will be diligently attempting to remove from you. Remember that maintaining itself is the primary focus of self-hate. It is clever, slippery, and tricky. In the beginning, it will fool you more often than not. And that is okay. It's not a contest. What you're learning in this work is to have compassion for yourself no matter what.

Going beyond the voices of self-hate to develop that compassion is immeasurably enhanced by a Recording and Listening Practice. R/L is the best tool we've found to assist us on this spiritual journey of waking up and ending suffering. For more information on this transformative practice, visit www.recordingandlistening.org.

Here are some suggestions to get you started:

Explore R/L by reading the sequel to this book, *What You Practice Is What You Have*.

Play the R/L card games in *What Universe Are You Creating?*

Ask yourself what are the things you've always wanted someone to say to you, but no one ever has. Ask the child inside you what it needs to hear you say. Make a recording. Tell yourself the things you've always wanted someone else to say. Include everything the child needs to hear to feel loved and appreciated. Listen to the recording every day. Add to it when you think of something else you want to hear.

Write love letters to yourself. Record and listen to them every day.

Think of at least one compassionate thing to do for yourself each day and do it.

Make a list of things you'd like to have and begin providing them for yourself.

Each time you give a gift to someone else, give something, even if it's little, to yourself.

Stop and appreciate yourself for every thought and act of kindness. Make an appreciation recording and listen to it often.

Say thank you to yourself when you do something kind.

Each time you receive a gift, give something, even if it's small, to someone else and really let yourself feel the joy of doing it.

Get comfortable saying I love you to yourself and say it many times each day. Make and listen to an I-love-you recording.

Take out pictures of yourself when you were little, frame them, place them in prominent places and let yourself begin to appreciate that little person.

Self-hating voices always lie! Each time you become aware of a self-hating thought or action, make a recording that reminds you of what is true. **Never record self-hating messages!**

And, of course, we would encourage a time of quiet and solitude each day (preferably a time of meditation) in order to be more present to yourself.

The only way out of this life of suffering is through the doorway of compassion.

"But how do I find the doorway?"

You can't find it because you are it. The moment there is nothing left of you but compassion, you are the doorway.

The door is wide open and you are free.

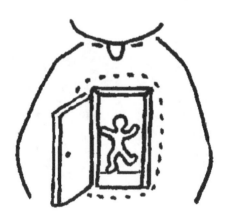

Work with Cheri Huber

To talk with Cheri call in to Open Air, her internet-based radio show. Archives of the show and instructions on how to participate are available at www.openairwithcherihuber.org.

To work with Cheri on an individual basis, sign up for her email classes at livingcompassion.org/schedule.

Visit www.recordingandlistening.org to learn about Recording and Listening, the practice that is Cheri's passion.

Visit cherihuber.com to access Cheri's latest interviews.

Cheri's books are available from your local independent bookstore, www.keepitsimple.org, and other online booksellers.

A Center for the Practice
of Zen Buddhist Meditation

Visit livingcompassion.org for more information on Zen Awareness Practice and the teachings of Cheri Huber.

- Find a schedule of retreats and workshops
- Find out more about virtual practice opportunities such as Reflective Listening, Virtual Meditation and Email Classes
- Access newsletters and blogs on Zen Awareness Practice
- Sign up for Recording and Listening Training
- Find out about our work in a community in Zambia. Read blogs with updates.

Contact
information@livingcompassion.org

There Is Nothing Wrong with You
An Extraordinary Eight-Day Retreat
based on the book
*There Is Nothing Wrong with You:
Going Beyond Self-Hate*
by Cheri Huber

Inside each of us is a "persistent voice of discontent." It is constantly critical of life, the world, and almost everythi··· we say and do. As children, in order to survive we learn listen to this voice and believe what it says.

This retreat is eight days of looking directly at how we are rejected and punished by the voices of self-hate and discovering how to let that go. Through a variety of exercises and periods of group processing, participants gain a clearer perspective on how they live their lives and on how to find compassion for themselves and others.

This work is challenging, joyous, fulfilling, scary, courageous, demanding, freeing, loving, kind, and compassionate— compassionate toward yourself and everyone you will ever know.

For information on attending, contact:
information@livingcompassion.org

WHAT UNIVERSE
ARE YOU CREATING?

ZEN AND THE ART OF
RECORDING AND LISTENING:
A 52-CARD DECK & GUIDEBOOK

Acceptance

CHERI HUBER & ASHWINI NARAYANAN
AUTHORS OF I DON'T WANT TO, I DON'T FEEL LIKE IT

What Universe Are You Creating? is a playful, powerful way
to learn the skill of Recording and Listening, a revolutionary
tool for practicing turning attention from incessant,
haranguing, karmically conditioned patterns of thought and
action to the peace of presence. Recording in your own voice
and then listening to kind words, encouragement,
inspirational readings, favorite songs, gratitude lists,
meditations—in short, being your own mentor—turns
attention away from the constant stream of negative self-
talk, robbing it of its power by revealing its illusory nature.

ISBN: 9780991596300